CATHOLIC AND CULTURAL BURIAL TRADITIONS IN LOUISIANA

This book is a guide for interested notaries, attorneys, funeral directors, church officials, and cemetery directors. It is not legal advice nor the practice of law. The author draws on his practical experience in the field as a cemetery director and as a commissioned Louisiana Civil Law Notary Public, but does not hold himself out to be an attorney at law. Those using any suggestions and forms are advised to confirm and update them with their own research. Use of this book constitutes full and voluntary acceptance of the risk of error, misapplication, or invalidity.

Any statement of "should" or "is advised" or similar is based on the author's personal and practical experience. It is not legal advice.

CATHOLIC AND CULTURAL BURIAL TRADITIONS IN LOUISIANA

A Guide to Faith, Heritage, and Sacred Practice

JOSHUA R. LEBLANC

Bayou State
PUBLISHING

For permission requests, contact:
Bayou State Publishing
P.O. Box 1049
Abbeville, LA 70511
Email: info@bayoustatepublishing.com
Website: bayoustatepublishing.com

ISBN: 978-1-970659-02-3

Printed in the United States of America
First Edition, 2025

Published by **Bayou State Publishing**
Youngsville, LA

Disclaimer:
The information contained in this book is provided for general educational and informational purposes only. Nothing in this book should be construed as, or relied upon as, legal advice. Laws and regulations vary by jurisdiction and are subject to change. Readers are strongly encouraged to consult with a qualified attorney before making any decisions or taking any action based on the material presented herein. The author and publisher expressly disclaim any liability for actions taken or not taken based on the contents of this book.

ABOUT THE AUTHOR

Joshua R. LeBlanc serves as the Executive Director of Holy Family Cemetery in New Iberia, Louisiana. He was ordained a Catholic deacon for the Diocese of Lafayette in 2016 and is currently assigned to St. Martin de Tours Catholic Church in St. Martinville.

Deacon LeBlanc brings a unique combination of theological insight, pastoral care, and administrative precision to the sacred work of cemetery management.

He holds a Master of Arts in Moral Theology and a +30 in Bioethics from Holy Apostles College and Seminary and is certified in Bioethics by the National Catholic Bioethics Center. He is currently pursuing a Doctorate in the field of Bioethics.

In addition to his ministry and administrative leadership. Deacon LeBlanc is a commissioned Civil Law Notary Public in and for the State of Louisiana and the owner of two small businesses – an IT firm and Chesterton's Fine Cigars in Youngsville, La. It is through this background that he shares his expertise in faith, ethics, and cemetery law.

Deacon LeBlanc also serves as a police chaplain and reserve police officer for the Youngsville and Abbeville Police Departments. He is also chaplain for the Military and Hospitaller Order of St. Lazarus of Jerusalem in the rank of Ecclesiastical Commander, whose mission is to serve the sick and dying. He is the Delegate for the Imperial Calcasieu Delegation and Vice Chancellor for Communications for the Grand Priory of America

As a deacon, he has ministered to grieving families for years, guiding them through the Catholic Church's teachings on death, burial, and resurrection. As a professional cemetery administrator, he has developed robust compliance systems rooted in Louisiana law, ensuring that every interment, fund, and record upholds both the dignity of the deceased and the legal obligations of the living.

Deacon LeBlanc is the author of *The Louisiana Cemetery Handbook:* Law, Compliance, and Administration and *The Louisiana Cemetery Form Book: Legal Documents, Templates, and Compliance Tools for Cemetery Authorities and Notaries Public*, the companion books in this series. Together, these works form the foundation of *The Louisiana Cemetery Authority Series*, a comprehensive legal and operational reference for religious and civil cemetery professionals throughout the state.

He and his wife, Annie, reside in Abbeville, Louisiana, with their cat Benedict.

THE LOUISIANA CEMETERY AUTHORITY SERIES

The Louisiana Cemetery Handbook: Law, Compliance, and Administration: A comprehensive guide to Louisiana cemetery law, Title 8 statutes, case law, and regulatory compliance.

The Louisiana Cemetery Forms Book: Documents, Templates, and Compliance Tools for Cemetery Authorities and Notaries Public. A companion volume containing practical forms, sample contracts, affidavits, and checklists for daily operations.

Catholic and Cultural Burial Traditions in Louisiana: A Guide to Faith, Heritage, and Sacred Practice. A comprehensive exploration of Louisiana's Catholic, Cajun, Creole, African American, and Native burial customs, offering theological insight, cultural history, and practical guidance for cemetery professionals and families.

Louisiana Cemetery Case Law: Jurisprudence, Practical Lessons, and Title 8 in the Courts. A clear and practical guide to Louisiana's major cemetery cases, this volume explains how courts interpret Title 8 in real-world disputes involving burial authority, disinterment, family cemeteries, undeveloped land sales, trust funds, and historic burial protections.

The Notary's Guide to Louisiana Cemetery Law: Authority, Documentation, and Practice Under Title 8. A practical reference that equips Louisiana notaries with clear, compliant language, clauses, and pastoral guidance for navigating cemetery ownership, interment rights, and Title 8 obligations in everyday notarial practice.

THE LOUISIANA CEMETERY HANDBOOK

Law, Compliance, and Administration

The *Louisiana Cemetery Handbook* is the state's most comprehensive and authoritative guide to the legal, historical, and operational foundations of cemetery management in Louisiana. Written for cemetery authorities, notaries public, attorneys, clergy, and municipal officials, it explains—in clear and practical language—**how Louisiana's unique burial laws work** and how they should be applied in everyday cemetery operations.

This essential volume includes:

- **A full explanation of Louisiana's cemetery laws**, including Title 8, Louisiana Civil Code, and relevant Administrative Code provisions.
- **Historical and cultural background** that illuminates why Louisiana's cemetery laws are distinct from those of any other state.
- **Detailed commentary on interment rights, perpetual care, abandonment procedures, dedication and removal, disinterment, merchandise trust laws, succession issues, and more.**
- **Best-practice guidelines** for cemetery operations, recordkeeping, trust fund compliance, and consumer protection.
- **Practical examples, case studies, and diagrams** to help cemetery personnel apply the law correctly.
- **Professional insights** informed by the author's experience in cemetery administration, notarial practice, and pastoral ministry.

TABLE OF CONTENTS

PART V – SPECIAL TOPICS

PREFACE

Louisiana's cemeteries are extraordinary. They are places where cultures converge, where faith is expressed in richly textured forms, and where families gather to honor the stories of their ancestors. Serving as a Catholic Cemetery Director in this unique landscape has shaped every page of this book.

I have walked with grieving families who brought Cajun French prayers, military honors, gospel hymns, Vietnamese incense, and Cajun French rosaries to the graveside. I have navigated complex questions about cremation, interment rights, Title 8 compliance, pet interment requests, cultural symbolism, and disputes between family members. I have witnessed how funeral traditions — whether Catholic or cultural — become a powerful source of comfort and identity.

This book was born from those experiences.

Its purpose is threefold:

1. **To help Catholic Cemetery Directors, clergy, and pastoral caregivers integrate Louisiana's cultural traditions with authentic Catholic teaching.**
2. **To help non-Catholic or secular cemetery managers understand — and respectfully adapt — Louisiana's diverse burial customs within their own operational frameworks.**
3. **To preserve and celebrate the rich funeral traditions of Louisiana's people for future generations.**

While specific chapters address specifically Catholic norms, canon law, and theological principles, much of this material applies broadly to any Cemetery Authority seeking to serve families with cultural sensitivity, pastoral compassion, and legal integrity.

The pages that follow are not abstract. They come from the ground — literally — from the sacred grounds of Louisiana's cemeteries. I hope that they will honor the memory of those who rest there and strengthen the ministry of all who care for them,

HOW TO USE THIS BOOK

This book is structured to serve the needs of **cemetery directors, clergy, funeral professionals, students, historians**, and **families**. Because Louisiana's burial culture blends Catholic theology with powerful cultural traditions, the book is organized into sections that allow readers to explore each dimension clearly and meaningfully.

For Catholic Cemetery Directors and Clergy

Chapters highlight:

- Canonical norms and Catholic burial theology
- Pastoral guidance for committal services
- Managing cultural expressions at gravesides
- Working with families across diverse traditions
- Issues of decorum, reverence, and Catholic identity
- Navigating conflicts and applying Church teaching with compassion

These readers should pay special attention to:

- **Chapters 1–7:** Theology and Catholic practice
- **Chapters 15–19:** Professional and pastoral application

For Civil, Municipal, or Interdenominational Cemetery Directors

While the book includes Catholic-specific content, most chapters are universally applicable:

- Cultural traditions (Chapters 8–14)
- Decoration and conduct guidelines
- Title 8 regulatory guidance
- Family dispute management
- Preservation and sacred memory
- Cultural sensitivity training

These cemeteries may adapt Catholic sections as needed.

For Families and General Readers

The cultural chapters offer a clear, beautifully woven overview of Louisiana's:

- Cajun, Creole, and Native funeral traditions
- Gospel, jazz, and musical funerals
- Iconography and symbolism
- Seasonal observances such as All Saints'

These readers will especially enjoy:

- **Chapters 8–14**
- **Ground Lessons** sidebars
- **Cultural Notes** sections

For Students, Historians, and Cultural Researchers

This book provides:

- Historical context for Louisiana burial practices
- Cultural anthropology of cemetery traditions
- Insights into folk religion, language, and identity
- Links between European Catholicism and African/Caribbean spiritual heritage

Sources are noted through:

- Scripture
- Catechism references (CCC)
- Canon law (CIC)
- Liturgical legislation (OCF)
- Louisiana statutes (La. R.S. Title 8)

Special Features of the Book

- **Cultural Notes** explain regional customs.
- **Ground Lessons** explore real burial situations and case studies.
- **Pastoral Insight** provides guidance for directors and clergy.
- **Inline citations** give clarity without interrupting the narrative flow.

Flexibility and Adaptation

Where Catholic requirements are specific, I note them clearly. Where cultural practices vary, I offer multiple approaches. Where legal obligations (Title 8) apply, they are explained accurately and accessibly.

Readers from any background will find material relevant to their work, heritage, and understanding of burial traditions in Louisiana.

INTRODUCTION

Cemeteries are more than final resting places — they are repositories of memory, culture, and faith. In Louisiana, where Catholic tradition, French and Spanish colonial heritage, African-American spirituality, Creole and Cajun customs, and Native American ancestry converge, cemeteries become a living tapestry of the people who shaped our land. They teach us who we were, who we are, and the beliefs we carry into death and beyond.

This book, *Catholic and Cultural Burial Traditions in Louisiana*, emerges from my experience as a Catholic Cemetery Director serving families across cultures, languages, histories, and traditions. Every day, I witness how grief expresses itself differently across communities — and how hope remains constant. Burial practices are not just practical necessities; they are acts of love, cultural identity, and theological expression.

While Louisiana is widely known for its rich Catholic heritage, especially in Acadiana and the river parishes, the truth is that our burial traditions draw from a much broader cultural well. Even in predominantly Catholic regions, families may bring African American gospel traditions, Caribbean influences, Protestant hymns, military customs, or French-Creole devotions to the graveside. Rather than seeing these practices as interruptions or deviations, I have come to understand them as beautiful expressions of the diverse communities we serve.

As such, **this book serves two primary audiences:**

CATHOLIC CEMETERY DIRECTORS AND PARISH LEADERS

Much of this text is written from the vantage point of Catholic cemetery management. Certain chapters address:

- Canonical norms
- Catholic liturgical practice
- The theology of Christian burial
- Cemetery conduct consistent with Catholic identity
- Pastoral sensitivity for clergy and cemetery staff
- How to integrate Louisiana's cultural expressions without compromising Catholic teaching

These sections respond directly to the practical realities I encounter as a Catholic Cemetery Director — questions about cremation, cultural rituals, second lines, images, pet interments, family disagreements, and Title 8 compliance.

NON-CATHOLIC, CIVIL, AND SECULAR CEMETERY PROFESSIONALS

Louisiana's cultural traditions do not stop at religious boundaries. Directors of interdenominational, municipal, or private cemeteries will find:

- Cultural insights
- Best practices for working with diverse communities
- Practical guidance on processions, decorations, and family expectations
- Historical context for Louisiana's burial customs
- Tools for navigating conflict, grief, and cultural nuance

While certain Catholic elements do not apply to non-Catholic cemeteries, **most chapters can be adapted easily.** Cultural sensitivity, respect for the dead, pastoral communication, and clear policy enforcement are universal principles, regardless of religious affiliation.

A Book Grounded in Lived Experience

This book is not merely academic. It is rooted in:

- countless graveside services,
- conversations with grieving families,
- pastoral moments in the midst of tragedy,
- annual All Saints' and All Souls' processions,
- the daily work of maintaining sacred grounds,
- and the complexity of the Louisiana Revised Statutes Title 8.

The chapters that follow draw from the rich cultural mosaic of Louisiana and the unchanging hope offered by Catholic teaching. Whether you direct a cemetery, minister to grieving families, lead a parish, study Louisiana culture, or simply seek to understand our burial heritage, this book will help you walk through cemeteries with new eyes.

A Living Tradition

Burial is one of the few practices that unites every Louisianian—Catholic, Protestant, Creole, Cajun, African American, Native American, Jewish, and secular alike. In a world where so much divides us, the cemetery reminds us of our shared humanity and our shared destiny. It is my hope that this book will help preserve, honor, and deepen these sacred traditions for generations to come.

KEY TO ABBREVIATIONS

Because this book references Catholic teaching, canon law, and liturgical documents, the following abbreviations are used consistently throughout the text:

Catechetical & Magisterial Documents

- **CCC** — *Catechism of the Catholic Church*
- **OCF** — *Order of Christian Funerals*
- **CIC** — *Codex Iuris Canonici* (1983 Code of Canon Law)

Civil Law (Louisiana)

- **La. R.S.** — *Louisiana Revised Statutes*
- **Title 8** — Cemetery Law within the Louisiana Revised Statutes
- **LAC** — *Louisiana Administrative Code*
- **LCB** — *Louisiana Cemetery Board*

PART 1

FOUNDATIONS OF BURIAL IN CATHOLIC AND LOUISIANA CULTURE

CHAPTER I

THE THEOLOGY OF CHRISTIAN BURIAL

Christian burial is rooted in a profound conviction: **every human life possesses an inherent dignity that does not end with death.** The body – created by God in His image and likeness, redeemed by Christ from our fallenness, and destined for resurrection like our savior – remains worthy of reverence even when the soul has departed. This conviction shapes every aspect of Catholic burial tradition in Louisiana, from the simple act of blessing the grave to the solemn procession that carries the deceased to their final resting place.

The Catholic Church has long understood burial not merely as a cultural practice, but as a work of mercy (cf. **Tobit 1:17**). To bury the dead is an act of charity, justice, and faith. It expresses hope in the Resurrection, acknowledges the communion we share with the deceased, and entrusts the departed soul to God's mercy. For this reason, the rituals surrounding death are considered some of the Church's most pastoral and tender moments of ministry.

The Human Person and the Dignity of the Body

Catholic teaching affirms that the human body is an essential aspect of the person, not merely a vessel, but part of our identity as a human being. The body is made in the image and likeness of God and is destined for eternal glory. Saint Paul reminds us that the body is a "temple of the Holy Spirit" **(1 Cor 6:19)**, a truth that continues even after death.

Thus, the Church insists that the body must be treated with respect at every stage: preparation, the vigil, funeral rites, and burial. This conviction lies behind the preference for burial of the body over cremation, the dignity of funeral liturgies, and the long tradition of consecrated cemeteries.

In Louisiana, this reverence is visible in the whitewashed tombs of south Louisiana, the above-ground family vaults of New Orleans, and the carefully tended rural graveyards of Acadiana. Whether simple or ornate, Catholic burial spaces testify to the sacredness of the human body and the community's responsibility to honor it as we await its resurrection.

Death as a Passage, Not an End

In Catholic understanding, death is not the extinction of the person but a passage from earthly life to eternal life. While the body dies, the soul remains. The Church proclaims in every funeral Mass: *"Life is changed, not ended."*

This perspective shapes the prayers, symbols, and customs found throughout Louisiana burial culture. The presence of holy water recalls baptism; incense signifies honor; the Paschal candle represents Christ's victory over death; and the rosary, vigil, and procession reflect a hope that extends beyond the grave.

Death rituals, therefore, are not only pastoral moments for the living but acts of faith in the enduring communion between the Church on earth (the Church Suffering) and the Church in heaven (the Church Triumphant).

The Communion of Saints

One of the most beautiful aspects of Christian burial is the affirmation that, in Christ, we remain united with the dead. This is not a metaphor but a doctrinal truth. The faithful departed remain members of the Body of Christ, deserving of prayer, remembrance, and love.

This belief is deeply embedded in Louisiana practice. Families maintain tombs for generations, return annually for the blessing of graves, and gather on All Saints and All Souls' Day to tend resting places and pray for the souls of the departed. These traditions express this truth: that the dead belong not only to the past but to the ongoing life of the Christian community.

The Hope of the Resurrection

The Resurrection of Jesus Christ is the cornerstone of Catholic teaching on burial. Because Christ rose from the dead, Christians believe they will rise as well, since Christ promised that we would share in His Resurrection **(Luke 14:14)**. This belief shapes everything from burial orientation and cemetery layout to liturgical prayer.

Traditionally, Christian graves were oriented toward the east — toward the rising sun — as a symbolic anticipation of Christ's return. While not universally practiced today, this symbolism still appears in many older Louisiana cemeteries, including some of the earliest French and Acadian settlements.

The final commendation in the funeral rite expresses this hope: *"May the angels lead you into Paradise."* This is not poetic sentiment but a proclamation of faith that the dead are entrusted to God and will one day rise in glory.

Burial as a Work of Mercy

Burying the dead has been recognized as a corporal work of mercy since the earliest days of the Church. In Louisiana, this duty took on particular urgency during epidemics, storms, or periods of poverty. Catholic communities historically built cemeteries adjacent to churches, not only for practical reasons but to ensure that even the poor and forgotten could be buried with dignity and to emphasize that the dead remain a part of the Church.

Today, Cemetery Authorities continue this apostolate. Whether caring for abandoned graves, assisting grieving families, or conducting committal services, they participate in the Church's mission of mercy.

The Liturgical Rhythm of Death and Burial

Catholic burial takes place within a liturgical rhythm shaped by centuries of tradition:

1. **The Vigil** (rosary or wake) — where the community gathers for prayer and remembrance.
2. **The Funeral Mass** — the Church's greatest prayer, offered for the soul of the deceased.
3. **The Rite of Committal** — the final act of entrusting the body to sacred ground.

Louisiana communities enrich these rites with unique cultural accents: French hymns, regional devotions, processions, and family participation that reflect local identity while remaining grounded in Catholic theology.

The Meaning of Sacred Ground

A cemetery is more than a resting place; **it is consecrated ground set apart for the dead.** Catholic tradition holds that burial in holy ground places the deceased within the heart of the Church. For this reason, the consecration of a cemetery is a solemn and significant act, often involving holy water, incense, and prayers invoking God's protection and blessing.

In Louisiana's Catholic culture, this sacredness is evident in the careful preservation of family tombs, the annual blessing of graves, and the communal sense that cemeteries are extensions of parish life.

CONCLUSION

The theology of Christian burial is not an abstract doctrine; it is a lived reality in Louisiana's Catholic and cultural landscape. From the reverence shown to the body to the celebration of All Saints Day and All Souls Day, from family tomb traditions to the rich liturgical rites of the Church, Louisiana's burial customs embody a deep and enduring faith.

Understanding these theological foundations is essential for clergy, Cemetery Authorities, cultural historians, and families seeking to preserve the sacred heritage entrusted to them.

In the chapters that follow, we will explore how these beliefs unfold in the consecration of cemeteries, the development of burial customs, and the diverse cultural traditions that make Louisiana's sacred ground unlike anywhere else in the world.

CHAPTER 2

THE CONSECRATION OF CEMETERIES

Cemeteries hold a privileged place within Catholic life, not because they contain the remains of the dead, but because they bear witness to the hope of the Resurrection. Consecrating a cemetery is a solemn act that sets aside a portion of the earth for sacred use, marking it as a place of prayer, remembrance, and Christian charity. In Louisiana, where faith and culture have shaped burial practices for centuries, the consecration of cemeteries carries a depth of meaning that unites theology, community identity, and pastoral care.

THE MEANING OF CONSECRATION

Consecration is a solemn act by which the Church dedicates land exclusively for the burial of the faithful (cf. **CIC 1205; CIC 1240 §1**). Unlike a simple blessing, which may be repeated or applied broadly, consecration establishes a permanent sacred character. Once a cemetery is consecrated, its soil becomes *ecclesia dormiens* — the "sleeping Church"— where the bodies of the faithful await the resurrection promised by Christ.

This act is not only spiritual but profoundly ecclesial. By consecrating a cemetery, the Church acknowledges the dignity of the human body, reinforces belief in the communion of the saints, and safeguards burial practices from secular misuse. It creates a space where the faithful can mourn, hope, and pray in continuity with centuries of Catholic tradition.

CULTURAL NOTE
Sacred Ground in Louisiana

Louisiana's earliest Catholic communities often placed cemeteries directly beside parish churches, following French and Spanish colonial practice. Even today, many rural and Acadiana cemeteries remain intimately tied to parish life—reminding the faithful that the Church on earth and the Church in heaven remain connected across generations.

Biblical and Theological Foundations

The consecration of burial ground reflects the biblical practice of setting aside places for sacred use. Abraham purchased the cave of Machpelah as a family burial site **(Gen 23)**. The prophets spoke of honoring the dead. The early Christians buried their faithful in consecrated catacombs, often near the graves of martyrs, believing that the bodies of the deceased shared in the sanctity of Christ's body.

Catholic teaching asserts that the bodies of the faithful become "temples of the Holy Spirit" **(1 Cor 6:19)** and will rise again **(Rom 6:5)**. Because of this, the land where they rest is worthy of dignity and protection. Consecration is the Church's way of proclaiming this dignity to all who enter the cemetery — even those outside the faith.

The Rite of Consecrating a Cemetery

Traditionally, the rite of consecrating a cemetery by a bishop, found in the Roman Ritual, is a formal ceremony to set the land apart for sacred use. The process typically involves the bishop or his designee reading a petition for consecration, processing around the perimeter and within the grounds, and sprinkling holy water while reciting prayers to purify the area from evil and bless it as a sacred resting place. (cf. **CIC 381; CIC 1207**).

Elements of the Rite Include:

- Procession around the perimeter of the cemetery
- A singing of the *Asperges me*
- Scripture readings (often **John 11** or **1 Thess 4**)
- Prayer of dedication
- Sprinkling of the entire area with holy water
- Blessing of the central cross or chapel
- A concluding prayer invoking perpetual peace

This ritual marks the cemetery not only as sacred ground but as a place of Christian hope, where the dead rest in anticipation of eternal life.

PASTORAL INSIGHT
The Bishop's Presence

The bishop's role emphasizes that Christian burial is not merely a family or cultural matter but a ministry of the whole Church. His presence at consecration underscores unity with the diocese and continuity with Catholic tradition.

Canonical Effects of Consecration

Once consecrated, a cemetery receives canonical protection:

- **It cannot be used for non-sacred functions** (cf. **CIC 1210**).
- **Its integrity must be preserved**, even in times of disaster or redevelopment (cf. **CIC 1208**).
- **Deconsecration requires a grave reason and a formal decree** (cf. **CIC 1212**).
- **Burials in consecrated ground carry spiritual benefit**, as they are linked to the prayer of the Church (cf. **CIC 1176 §3; CCC 2300**).

These protections serve both theological and pastoral purposes, ensuring that sacred ground remains dignified, peaceful, and free of commercial or secular encroachment.

GROUND LESSONS
When Cemeteries Move

Throughout Louisiana's history – after hurricanes, floods, and coastal shifts – parishes have sometimes been forced to relocate cemeteries. Canon law requires that the sacred character of the old site be preserved until the remains are reverently transferred and the ground formally deconsecrated. These events become moments of communal mourning, memory, and reaffirmation of faith.

Local Traditions in Consecration

Louisiana's consecration rituals often include distinctive elements not mandated by liturgical law but deeply woven into local culture:

- **Processions with French hymns** such as *"J'irai la voir un jour."*
- **Blessing of family tombs** during the same ceremony.
- **Community participation**, especially in small parishes, where families helped build the cemetery.
- **Use of holy water from parish baptismal fonts** symbolizes the link between baptism and burial.
- **Annual re-blessings** during All Saints and All Souls observances.

These practices reflect Louisiana's blend of Catholic devotion and cultural identity.

The Consecration of Sections and Crypts

In larger cemeteries — especially in New Orleans, Baton Rouge, Lafayette, and the River Parishes — Cemetery Authorities often request consecration of:

- Mausoleum crypts
- Columbarium niches
- Veterans' sections
- Children's or infant burial areas
- Priest or religious sections

- Newly developed expansions

Consecration may be performed on each new phase of construction or on dedicated sections within a larger cemetery. The rites are adaptable and allow for pastoral sensitivity, particularly when blessing areas intended for miscarried infants or the poor.

PASTORAL INSIGHT
Consecrating a Columbarium

Even though cremation was historically discouraged, the Church now permits it, provided the ashes are reverently interred (cf. **CIC 1176 §3**; Instruction *Ad resurgendum cum Christo*, 2016). Consecrating a columbarium ensures that cremated remains receive the same dignity as bodily remains.

RESPECT FOR CONSECRATED GROUND

Once consecrated, the cemetery must be maintained in a manner consistent with its sacred character. This includes:

- Proper landscaping and cleanliness
- Protection against vandalism
- Prevention of inappropriate commercial activity
- Ensuring reverent conduct by visitors
- Maintaining records of who is interred

In Louisiana's cultural context—where cemeteries are gathering places during All Saints' Day and other festivals – authorities must balance hospitality with respect.

CULTURAL NOTE
All Saints' Day as a Renewal of Consecration

In many communities, the blessing of graves on November 1 functions as an annual renewal of consecration. Families clean and whitewash tombs, replace flowers, and participate in prayers led by clergy. This day reinforces the cemetery's identity as a sacred space and unifies the community around its departed loved ones.

Conclusion

Consecration transforms a plot of land into holy ground—an outward sign of the Church's faith in the Resurrection and her enduring care for the faithful departed. In Louisiana, consecrated cemeteries stand as spiritual landmarks, cultural memorials, and pastoral centers where faith and heritage meet.

The rite is at once ancient and living, shaped by canon law, enriched by local tradition, and animated by the Catholic belief that the dead remain cherished members of the Church. As the chapters ahead will show, this sacred foundation supports the rich tapestry of Louisiana burial practice—from funeral rites and cultural customs to preservation, pastoral ministry, and cemetery stewardship.

CHAPTER 3

CIVIL LAW HERITAGE AND ITS INFLUENCE ON BURIAL

Louisiana stands alone among the states in its civil law foundation – a legal heritage shaped by France, Spain, Catholic sacramental theology, and centuries of cultural development. This distinctive legal environment profoundly affects how cemeteries are operated, how burial rights are transferred, and how the resting places of the dead are protected.

Understanding Louisiana burial traditions requires understanding Louisiana law. Here, property rights, family succession, servitudes, and cemetery dedication follow principles unlike those found anywhere else in the United States. These Civil Law foundations do not merely govern cemeteries – they reflect a worldview in which family, land, and memory are intimately connected.

THE CIVIL LAW TRADITION COMES TO LOUISIANA

Louisiana's legal system is rooted in a blend of French and Spanish colonial law, refined through the **Digest of 1808**, the **Civil Code of 1825**, and later the **Revised Civil Code of 1870**. Unlike common law jurisdictions shaped by judicial precedent, Louisiana's civil law emphasizes:

- Codified statutes
- Precise definitions of property rights
- Strong family protection
- A preference for written agreements
- The concept of **servitudes** – rights attached to property rather than people

This heritage shapes burial law in several unique ways. For example, cemetery dedication creates a **perpetual public servitude of use**, a concept unknown in many common law states. Ownership of land does not grant unlimited authority over it; once dedicated as a cemetery, the land becomes a protected, semi-sacred legal category.

CULTURAL NOTE
Why Louisiana Cemeteries Look Different

Above-ground tombs, family crypts, and long rows of heavy masonry vaults are not simply architectural preferences—they reflect the influence of European Catholic burial customs, combined with French and Spanish legal norms governing family property and succession.

Dedication and the Perpetual Servitude of Use

In Louisiana, once land is dedicated as a cemetery, it ceases to function as ordinary private property. Instead, it becomes burdened with a perpetual **servitude of public use** (cf. **La. R.S. 8:304 – 306**). This means:

- The owner can't freely repurpose the land.
- Families have rights of access and visitation.
- Interments cannot be disturbed except under strict legal procedures.
- The cemetery must remain a place of burial until the dedication is formally removed.

This legal structure mirrors the theological understanding of sacred ground (cf. **CIC 1210**). Even when a cemetery is privately owned, the law treats it as a place held in trust for the dead and for their families.

PASTORAL INSIGHT
Civil Law Mirrors Catholic Sensibilities

The concept of a perpetual servitude of use resonates deeply with Catholic burial theology. Both see burial grounds as places permanently set apart – spaces where the dead rest in hope and the living maintain a solemn bond of memory.

Family Rights and Succession Principles

Louisiana succession law greatly influences burial practice. Because cemeteries themselves are considered **immovable property** (cf. **La. R.S. 8:1**), the ownership of rights of use passes according to the Civil Code's rules governing immovables.

But Louisiana law adds an additional dimension: **the right of burial is a real right distinct from ordinary land ownership.**

Under Louisiana's intestate succession:

- A spouse acquires a **vested right of use** in empty cemetery spaces belonging to their deceased spouse (cf. **La. R.S. 8:805**).
- Children or descendants inherit burial rights when no spouse survives.
- If there are no descendants, burial rights pass to siblings, parents, or nearest relatives according to the Civil Code's order of inheritance.

This structure reflects Louisiana's strong commitment to family identity, shared memory, and continuity across generations—a feature deeply aligned with both Catholic theology and local culture.

GROUND LESSONS
When Families Disagree

Disputes over who may be buried in a family tomb are common across Louisiana. Because burial rights can exist independently of property ownership, courts often rely on family custom, historical patterns of interment, and "implied consent" to determine rightful use. These situations require Cemetery Authorities to proceed cautiously and, when necessary, advise families to seek legal counsel.

The Civil Code's Impact on Burial Customs

Several distinctive features of Louisiana law influence everyday burial practices:

Above-Ground Tombs

Above-ground burial became widespread not only because of cultural import but also because Louisiana civil law historically treated family tombs as immovable constructions, affording strong protections against alteration or removal.

Family Tombs as Collective Property

Louisiana recognizes the concept of **collective** or **co-owned** family tombs, which may pass intact through generations, often without formal title transfer. Family usage serves as practical evidence of ownership.

Burial Instructions and Donations

Because civil law strongly emphasizes written acts, many families formalize burial instructions through notarized declarations or donations of burial rights, even though cemetery conveyances need not be in authentic form (cf. **La. R.S. 8:812**).

Transfer Restrictions

The Civil Code's protection of family property discourages the sale of family tombs outside the family line — reinforcing cultural norms that view burial spaces as heritage, not commodities.

The Development of Louisiana's Cemetery Statutes (Title 8)

Louisiana Revised Statutes Title 8 was enacted to harmonize Civil Law principles with the practical needs of modern cemetery administration. Title 8 incorporates:

- Civil Code concepts of ownership and servitudes
- Canonical notions of sacred ground
- Consumer protection principles
- Requirements for perpetual care and trust funds
- Rules for dedication and de-dedication
- Procedures for disinterment and relocation

Title 8 also protects families from arbitrary cemetery actions by requiring:

- Notice of significant changes
- Recordkeeping of interments
- Restrictions on disturbance of remains
- Clear procedures for abandonment, renovation, and removal of dedication

In this way, Title 8 serves as a bridge between civil law, cultural expectation, and pastoral responsibility.

CULTURAL NOTE
Why Louisiana Has Stronger Cemetery Laws

Hurricane-prone regions, floodplains, and cultural attachment to family tombs pushed legislators to create laws that go far beyond what other states require. The result is a unique legal framework that safeguards cemeteries as both sacred spaces and historic resources.

Civil Law and Catholic Canon Law: A Cooperative Tension

Louisiana burial practice operates at the intersection of two legal systems:

- **Civil law**, governing property, succession, ownership, and contract
- **Canon law**, governing sacred ground, liturgical practice, and ecclesial oversight

While civil law ensures stability and public order, canon law ensures that burial practices reflect the Church's theology and pastoral care. Conflicts occasionally arise – for example, when a civil requirement for relocation intersects with canonical norms regarding consecrated ground (cf. **CIC 1212; CIC 1243**).

Cemetery Authorities must be attentive to both systems, especially in Catholic cemeteries where the bishop retains oversight of sacred places (cf. **CIC 381; CIC 1207**).

PASTORAL INSIGHT
Working Within Two Legal Systems

Cemetery staff often serve as intermediaries between grieving families, civil procedures, and canonical obligations. Clear communication, accurate records, and awareness of both civil and ecclesial requirements are essential.

The Living Tradition of Civil Law Burial Culture

Louisiana's Civil Law heritage is not merely historical — it actively shapes present-day burial culture:

- Family tombs preserve memory across generations.
- Cemeteries remain centers of community identity.
- All Saints' Day observances continue to reinforce burial rights and family lineage.
- Canonical and civil principles together protect the dignity of the deceased.

The result is a distinctive legal–spiritual ecosystem where civil law supports theological truth and culture enriches legal understanding.

GROUND LESSONS
The Role of Custom

In many Louisiana burial disputes, courts rely heavily on **custom,** who maintains the tomb, who is buried there, and who historically made decisions. Custom often carries the same weight as a formal title, a uniquely Civil Law feature.

CONCLUSION

Louisiana's Civil Law heritage provides the legal backbone of its burial culture. The interplay between codified law, Catholic theology, and deeply rooted family customs creates a distinctive environment that honors the dead, protects families, and maintains the sacredness of burial grounds.

This chapter forms the foundation for understanding the chapters ahead – particularly Louisiana's Catholic rites, cultural traditions, and the responsibilities of Cemetery Authorities within the state's unique legal framework.

PART II

CATHOLIC BURIAL PRACTICES IN LOUISIANA

CHAPTER 4

CATHOLIC FUNERAL RITES IN PRACTICE

The Catholic funeral rites are among the Church's most consoling pastoral ministries. Rooted in Scripture, tradition, and centuries of faith, these rites express three essential truths: the dignity of the human person, the hope of the Resurrection, and the communion that binds the living and the dead. In Louisiana — where Catholic culture blends with French, Creole, African American, and Native traditions — the funeral rites take on a uniquely local character while remaining faithful to the Church's universal liturgy.

This chapter explores the structure, purpose, and pastoral meaning of the Catholic funeral rites as they are commonly practiced throughout the state.

THE STRUCTURE OF CATHOLIC FUNERAL RITES

The **Order of Christian Funerals (OCF)** outlines three principal moments:

1. **The Vigil (Wake)**
2. **The Funeral Liturgy (Mass or Funeral Liturgy Outside Mass)**
3. **The Rite of Committal**

These rites reflect a journey — from grief to hope, from community gathering to liturgical prayer, and finally to burial in sacred ground. The Church's intention is not simply to "hold a service," but to accompany the family through grief with prayer, remembrance, and the proclamation of Christ's victory over death (cf. OCF, General Introduction).

CULTURAL NOTE
The Louisiana Sequence

In many Catholic communities in Acadiana and along the bayou parishes, the traditional sequence often includes:

- a rosary prayed (sometimes prayed in Cajun French),
- communal food gatherings at home,
- visits from extended family and neighbors,
- a funeral Mass filled with local hymns or *Ave Maria* sung in French, and a graveside procession accompanied by family prayers.

While not official components of the liturgy, these practices are deeply woven into Louisiana Catholic life.

The Vigil (Wake)

The **Vigil for the Deceased** is the Church's first and often most personal moment in the funeral rites. Held at a funeral home, church, or family home, it includes:

- **Scripture readings**
- **Prayers** for the deceased and family
- The **rosary**, frequently in French in certain parishes
- Opportunities for **storytelling and remembrance**

The OCF teaches that Vigil is the ideal time for eulogies or personal remembrances–not during the Funeral Mass (cf. **OCF 27**). Louisiana families often use this moment to share memories, music, or cultural elements reflecting the life of the deceased.

PASTORAL INSIGHT
The Power of Presence

At the Vigil, the Church accompanies the family in their grief before entering into the liturgical celebration of hope. Clergy and Cemetery Authorities who attend or offer prayers at the Vigil often form lasting pastoral relationships with families.

THE FUNERAL MASS

The **Funeral Mass** is the central liturgy of the Catholic funeral rites. The Church celebrates the paschal mystery – the dying, death, and resurrection of Christ – and prays for the soul of the deceased (cf. **CIC 1176 §2**).

KEY ELEMENTS INCLUDE:

The Reception of the Body

The body (or cremated remains, when permitted) is sprinkled with holy water, recalling baptism, and covered with a **white pall**, symbolizing the dignity given at baptism.

The Liturgy of the Word

Scripture readings proclaim God's promise of eternal life. Louisiana families often choose readings that reflect their cultural heritage, including French or bilingual readings in some communities.

The Liturgy of the Eucharist

The Funeral Mass is the Church's greatest prayer for the dead. Offering Mass for the deceased expresses faith in Christ's sacrifice made present on the altar.

The Final Commendation

Incense is used as a sign of honor and prayer rising before God. The invitation, *"Saints of God, come to their aid...,"* expresses communion with the heavenly Church.

GROUND LESSONS
When the Church Avoids Eulogies at Mass

Many families expect a eulogy during the Funeral Mass. However, the Church's norms are explicit: personal remembrances belong at the Vigil or reception (cf. **OCF 27**). This often surprises families accustomed to Protestant or secular funeral formats.

Pastoral explanation is essential — and greatly appreciated when offered with sensitivity.

FUNERAL LITURGY OUTSIDE OF MASS

In situations where Mass cannot be celebrated — such as when the deceased was not Catholic, when circumstances make the Mass impractical, or when a priest is unavailable — the Church provides the **Funeral Liturgy Outside of Mass** (cf. **OCF 177–203**).

This rite includes:

- Reception of the body
- Scripture readings
- Prayers for the deceased
- Final commendation

In many Louisiana communities where priests serve multiple parishes, this option is often used, especially for weekday funerals.

The Rite of Committal

The **Rite of Committal** takes place at the grave, tomb, mausoleum, or columbarium. It is the final act of the Church's care for the deceased (cf. **OCF 204**).

Elements of the Committal:

- Invitation and Scripture passage
- Prayer of committal
- Intercessions
- The Lord's Prayer
- Blessing of the grave or crypt
- Concluding blessing

The committal connects the Funeral Mass to the burial. It is short, but deeply moving – especially in Louisiana, where the cemetery is often central to family identity.

CULTURAL NOTE
The Procession to the Cemetery

In older Acadiana communities, processions, on foot or in slow-moving vehicles, follow the hearse to the cemetery. Historic New Orleans neighborhoods also preserve vestiges of the procession tradition, particularly around parish churches and family tombs.

The Role of Music in the Sacred Rites

Music is integral to Catholic funerals and the preferred option when available (cf. **OCF 30**). In Louisiana, music often reflects local culture:

- French hymns
- African American spirituals
- Bagpipes in areas with Irish heritage
- Organ accompaniment for traditional Latin hymns
- Brass instruments in New Orleans Catholic parishes
- "Nearer, My God, to Thee" or *Le Salut* during procession

While secular songs are prohibited during sacred rites, they may be appropriate at the Vigil or a family gathering.

PASTORAL INSIGHT

Honoring Music Requests

Pastors and Cemetery Authorities often help families understand where beloved songs should be placed. A favorite Cajun ballad, for example, may beautifully come after the Vigil or after the committal, while not appropriate for Mass.

Cremation within the Funeral Rites

Although the Church prefers burial of the body (cf. **CIC 1176 §3; CCC 2301**), cremation is permitted if it is not chosen for reasons contrary to the faith.

Louisiana has embraced cremation at a rate higher than previous generations, partly due to cost, mobility, and changing family patterns.

KEY POINTS:

- If possible, the body should be present at the Funeral Mass before cremation.
- If cremation occurs first, the ashes must be treated with the same dignity as a body.
- Ashes must be interred in a cemetery or columbarium – not scattered or kept at home (cf. *Ad resurgendum cum Christo,* 2016).

Many Louisiana Catholic cemeteries now include consecrated columbaria to ensure proper care of cremated remains.

PASTORAL SENSITIVITY AND CULTURAL EXPRESSION

Louisiana Catholics bring a tapestry of cultural traditions to funerals:

- Cajun storytelling
- Creole food at post-funeral gatherings
- Second-line elements among New Orleans Catholics
- French rosaries
- Devotions to various saints
- Native American rituals incorporated before or after the Church's sacred rites

These traditions are not contrary to Catholic practice when placed in the correct liturgical or pastoral moment.

GROUND LESSONS
Where Culture and the Sacred Meet

A second-line celebration after the Rite of Committal is perfectly legitimate as an expression of cultural celebration of life, **so long as the sacred rites themselves remain intact.** The Church embraces cultural beauty but protects the dignity of the sacred liturgy.

The Priest, Deacon, and Lay Minister's Roles

Each minister has specific responsibilities (cf. **OCF 14 - 18**):

- **Priest:** presides at Funeral Mass, committal, and confers blessings
- **Deacon:** presides at Vigil, Funeral Outside Mass, and committal, assists the priest at Mass, and confers blessings
- **Lay ministers:** lead Vigil prayers, assist families, serve in music ministry

Cemetery Authorities often function as essential pastoral partners, guiding families through decisions regarding burial, timing, and cultural expectations.

Family Participation

Families may participate by:

- Reading Scripture
- Bringing up the gifts
- Selecting music
- Sharing memories at the Vigil
- Leading rosaries
- Carrying the casket

Louisiana families frequently bring traditional objects — photos, rosaries, and prayer cards — to display at the Vigil. These should never be placed on the coffin during Mass, preserving the rite's sacred structure.

Conclusion

The Catholic funeral rites blend sacred theology, pastoral care, and cultural expression into a unified act of mercy. In Louisiana, these rites take on a distinctive character shaped by history, faith, and community identity.

At their heart, they proclaim the same enduring truth: that Christ has conquered death and that the deceased remain united with the Church, entrusted to God's eternal mercy.

The following chapters will explore how these rites connect with Catholic cemetery principles, local traditions, and the vibrant cultural landscape of Louisiana.

CHAPTER 5

CATHOLIC CEMETERIES AND THEIR CANONICAL PRINCIPLES

Catholic cemeteries are not simply burial grounds – they are extensions of the Church's life, sacred places where faith, memory, and community converge. Canon law treats cemeteries as holy places, set apart for the faithful departed and entrusted to the care of the Church so that the dead may rest in a place marked by dignity, prayer, and hope.

In Louisiana, this canonical vision blends naturally with cultural practice. The whitewashed tombs, family vaults, All Saints gatherings, and community processions all reflect a deep respect for sacred ground that is both ecclesial and cultural. Understanding Catholic cemetery principles provides the foundation for faithful stewardship of these holy places.

SACRED PLACES IN CANON LAW

Canon law defines sacred places as locations designated for worship, prayer, or the burial of the faithful (cf. **CIC 1205**). These places are set apart by **dedication or blessing**, making them distinct from ordinary land.

KEY CANONICAL CHARACTERISTICS OF SACRED PLACES:

- They are regulated by ecclesiastical authority (cf. **CIC 1206 - 1207**).
- They must remain suitable for worship or sacred use (cf. **CIC 1210**).
- They enjoy special protection against profanation or misuse (cf. **CIC 1211**).

Catholic cemeteries fall under this classification because burial is not merely a civil act – it is a liturgical and theological moment linked to baptism, the Communion of Saints, and the hope of resurrection.

CULTURAL NOTE
Sacred Ground and Community Identity

In Louisiana, parish cemeteries often stand in the heart of community life. Many parishes founded by French, Spanish, African, and Acadian settlers established their cemeteries adjacent to the church, symbolizing unity with the worshiping community and the bond between the living and the dead.

THE PURPOSE OF A CATHOLIC CEMETERY

The Church's tradition identifies three principal purposes of a Catholic cemetery:

1. **A Place of Prayer**
   The faithful departed remain members of the Church. Their resting places are spaces where the living pray for the dead and commend them to God's mercy.
2. **A Witness to Faith**
   The cemetery visibly proclaims belief in the resurrection of the body and the communion of saints.
3. **A Sanctuary of Dignity**
   The cemetery ensures the body is treated with reverence, safeguarded from desecration, and placed in an environment consistent with Christian belief (cf. **CCC 2300**).

Catholic cemeteries embody the Church's mission to accompany the faithful from baptism to burial, offering a final sign of hope in Christ.

Governance of Catholic Cemeteries

Catholic cemeteries are typically under the supervision of the diocesan bishop, who has authority over sacred places within the diocese (cf. **CIC 381; CIC 1207**). The bishop may entrust cemetery administration to:

- Parishes
- Religious orders
- Lay cemetery associations
- Catholic cemetery corporations

Regardless of the administrative structure, the bishop retains oversight to ensure that burial practices conform to Catholic teaching.

Canonical Responsibilities Include:

- Maintaining reverence and order
- Ensuring proper burial and committal practices
- Protecting sacred space from misuse
- Safeguarding the rights of families
- Regulating cremation and interment of ashes
- Approving the construction of mausoleums or columbaria in sacred places

The bishop's pastoral authority ensures that cemeteries remain truly Catholic in identity and practice.

> **PASTORAL INSIGHT**
> **When a "Catholic Cemetery" Isn't Officially Catholic**
>
> Some cemeteries in Louisiana bear historic names like "St. ___ Cemetery," even though they are no longer owned or administered by the Church. Without diocesan approval, a cemetery cannot claim canonical status – even if it "looks Catholic." Cemetery Authorities should be attentive when describing the cemetery to avoid implying canonical oversight where none exists

Burial Rights in Catholic Cemeteries

The Church teaches that Christians "are to be buried in a church cemetery" when possible (cf. **CIC 1180 §1**). Parishioners, clergy, and, often, non-Catholic family members may be granted burial in a Catholic cemetery in accordance with diocesan norms.

Who May Be Buried in a Catholic Cemetery?

- **Catholics**
- **Catechumens** (cf. **CIC 1183 §1**)
- **Members of non-Catholic Christian communities** whose intention or family connection warrants it (cf. **CIC 1183 §3**)
- **Non-baptized spouses or family members**, as permitted by diocesan policy

The Church discourages denying burial, except in grave circumstances, such as when the deceased publicly rejected the Catholic faith.

> **CULTURAL NOTE**
> **Inclusivity in Louisiana Parish Cemeteries**
>
> Historically, many Louisiana parish cemeteries included non-Catholic relatives, civil leaders, benefactors, and community members because the parish cemetery was often the only cemetery available. This culturally rooted openness continues today under diocesan norms.

Cremation, Ashes, and Catholic Cemeteries

While burial of the body is preferred (cf. **CIC 1176 §3**), cremation is permitted if not chosen for reasons contrary to Christian teaching. Catholic cemeteries must ensure that cremated remains:

- Are interred in a grave, niche, or mausoleum
- Are not scattered, divided, or kept at home (cf. *Ad resurgendum cum Christo*, 2016)
- Receive the same respect as a body

Many Louisiana Catholic cemeteries now include:

- Consecrated columbaria
- Niche walls
- Cremation sections within family tombs
- Shared crypt spaces for spouses choosing cremation

These practices ensure that cremated remains are treated with dignity and entrusted to sacred ground.

GROUND LESSONS
Misunderstandings About Ashes

A common pastoral issue is families wishing to scatter ashes in bayous, hunting camps, or family property. While these gestures express good intentions, they conflict with Catholic teaching, which requires ashes to be committed to consecrated ground. Cemetery Authorities often help families navigate these difficult conversations with compassion and clarity.

Canonical Requirements for Construction and Renovation

Canonical norms protect the integrity of the cemetery when new structures are added, or existing ones are modified (cf. **CIC 1210 - 1211**). Projects that may require diocesan oversight include:

Mausoleum construction

- Columbarium installation
- Major expansion of burial sections
- Removal or relocation of tombs
- Renovation that affects the sacred character of the space

The bishop may insist on proper design, reverence, and compliance with liturgical norms.

COMMON LOUISIANA FEATURES REQUIRING OVERSIGHT:

- Community mausoleums
- Acadian-style family vaults
- Latin cross monuments
- Priest burial sections
- Niches added within historic structures

These features reflect cultural expression but must remain consistent with canonical expectations.

Conduct Within Catholic Cemeteries

Because Catholic cemeteries are sacred places, canon law requires reverence and appropriate conduct (cf. **CIC 1210**). Dioceses often establish rules addressing:

- Respectful visitation
- Prohibition of disruptive behavior
- Restrictions on secular activities
- Appropriate decoration and maintenance
- Behavior during processions and rites
- Photography or filming during sacred rites
- Preservation of artifacts and historic tombs

These policies protect the dignity of the deceased and maintain the cemetery's sacred character for all who visit.

CULTURAL NOTE
All Saints' Day as a Model of Reverence

Louisiana's All Saints' Day traditions – cleaning, decorating, praying, and blessing the graves – serve as a living example of the reverence expected in Catholic cemeteries year-round. These practices reinforce both canonical principles and local identity.

The Spiritual Significance of Catholic Cemeteries

Beyond their legal and administrative structure, Catholic cemeteries embody profound spiritual meaning:

- **Places of Hope:** They proclaim Christ's promise of resurrection.
- **Places of Memory:** They preserve the identity and history of families and communities.
- **Places of Communion:** They unite the living and the dead in prayer.
- **Places of Mercy:** They care for the poor, the forgotten, and the abandoned.

In Louisiana, these elements come alive in parish gatherings, French prayers spoken beside graves, and families tending tombs passed down through generations.

PASTORAL INSIGHT
A Cemetery as a Parish's "Silent Parishioners"

We can think of a cemetery as the parish of those who have already crossed through the veil. Their presence shapes the community's spiritual identity, reminding the faithful of their destiny and calling them to prayer.

Conclusion

Catholic cemeteries are sacred places entrusted to the Church's care, grounded in canon law, animated by theology, and enriched by cultural tradition. In Louisiana, their significance is felt not only in liturgical rites but in the daily life of communities that honor the dead with reverence, devotion, and continuity.

These canonical principles guide the stewardship of sacred ground, ensuring that Catholic cemeteries remain places of dignity, hope, and sacred memory for generations to come.

CHAPTER 6

ALL SAINTS AND ALL SOULS TRADITIONS

Few traditions capture the heart of Louisiana Catholic culture more vividly than All Saints Day and All Souls Day. In many parts of the world, these feasts pass quietly, marked by a Mass or simple prayer. But in Louisiana – particularly in Acadiana and the river parishes – these days are living, communal feasts of faith. Families gather in the cemetery, tombs are whitewashed, flowers are placed with care, and clergy walk among the graves blessing them with holy water.

These traditions form a bridge between the sacred liturgy, family identity, and cultural memory. They express a theology rooted in the Communion of Saints (cf. **CCC 946 - 959**) and reveal a uniquely Louisiana way of honoring the dead with love, reverence, and hope.

The Liturgical Significance of Nov. 1-2

The Church teaches that **All Saints Day (Nov. 1)** honors the countless holy men and women who now dwell in the presence of God. **All Souls Day (Nov. 2)** is devoted to praying for the faithful departed who are being purified in the mercy of God (cf. **CCC 1030 - 1032**).

Together, these days proclaim:

- The victory of Christ
- The communion between heaven, earth, and the dead
- The Christian hope of resurrection
- The duty to pray for the souls of the departed

In Catholic theology, these feasts highlight a profound truth: **death does not sever the bonds of love**, and prayer for the dead is a spiritual work of mercy.

> **CULTURAL NOTE**
> **"La Toussaint"**
>
> In French Louisiana, All Saints Day was traditionally called *"La Toussaint,"* literally "All Saints." Families traveled miles – often by boat, horseback, or wagon – to reach the cemetery. Prayer, family gathering, French hymns, and the blessing of graves marked the day.

Preparing the Cemetery: Cleaning, Whitewashing, and Flowers

The weeks leading up to All Saints Day bring a flurry of activity in Catholic cemeteries across Louisiana. Families visit their ancestral plots to:

- Sweep and scrub the tomb
- Repaint or whitewash masonry
- Replace broken decorations
- Trim grass and remove debris
- Place new flowers (often chrysanthemums)
- Restore family statues or crucifixes

These actions express more than aesthetic care — they symbolize spiritual preparation, a renewal of reverence toward sacred ground.

Whitewashing, especially in Acadiana, became a communal event. Families would wash and paint entire rows of tombs, turning cemeteries into stunning vistas of bright white, reflecting the purity and hope proclaimed on All Saints Day.

> **GROUND LESSONS**
> **“The Cemetery Must Be Ready for the Saints”**
>
> Older generations often taught children that the cemetery had to be clean “so the saints could walk among the tombs.” This catechetical folk teaching reveals a beautiful truth: All Saints’ Day is not about death but about holiness, hope, and community.

The Blessing of the Graves

One of Louisiana’s most cherished Catholic traditions is the **Blessing of the Graves**, customarily held after Mass on All Saints Day. Clergy process through the cemetery, reading Scripture and blessing each grave with holy water.

TYPICAL ELEMENTS INCLUDE:

- Entrance hymn or French canticles
- Psalm or Scripture reading
- Prayers for the dead
- Incense at parish cemeteries with rich liturgical traditions
- Sprinkling of holy water on each grave
- Recitation of the rosary, often in French

In some parishes, each family remains at their tomb while the clergy travel from grave to grave. In others, the entire congregation processes together behind the priest or deacon.

Louisiana's strong cultural memory has preserved this tradition even in communities where it had faded elsewhere.

PASTORAL INSIGHT
A Unifying Celebration

All Saints' Day often draws Catholics who may not regularly attend church. The cemetery becomes a place of reconciliation, healing, and renewed connection with both faith and family.

ALL SOULS DAY: PRAYING FOR THE FAITHFUL DEPARTED

While All Saints Day is a festive celebration, **All Souls Day (Nov. 2)** carries a more contemplative tone. The Church invites the faithful to pray for the souls undergoing purification in purgatory (cf. **CCC 1030 – 1032**). The faithful offer:

- Requiem Masses
- Visits to the cemetery
- Rosaries and litanies for the dead
- Lighting of candles
- Indulgenced prayers for souls in purgatory (cf. *Enchiridion of Indulgences*)

In Louisiana, many families return to the cemetery on All Souls Day, sometimes bringing candles to place atop tombs – a tradition reminiscent of Catholic Europe.

CULTURAL NOTE
Lighting the Way

Placing candles on tombs has long symbolized the light of Christ guiding the faithful departed. In some Creole communities, dozens of candles illuminated the cemetery after sunset on All Souls' Day, creating a breathtaking "sea of light."

Family Gatherings and Community Bonds

For many Louisiana families, All Saints' Day functions like a sacred family reunion. Generations gather around the family tomb to pray, reminisce, and reconnect. The day reinforces:

- The continuity of family identity
- The value of tradition
- The dignity of ancestors
- The importance of faith

Some families bring meals to share after the blessing. In early Louisiana, families picnicked near the cemetery, blending social custom with sacred remembrance.

These practices underscore a foundational belief: honoring the dead strengthens the living.

Music, Hymns, and Processional Traditions

The musical life of Louisiana enriches All Saints Day. Depending on the region, one might hear:

- French hymns, such as *"J'irai la voir un jour"*
- Cajun-French rosary chants
- African American spirituals
- Processional hymns accompanied by brass bands in historic urban parishes such as New Orleans
- Simple chanted psalms in rural areas

Music elevates the blessing of graves, transforming the cemetery into a place of living prayer.

GROUND LESSONS
The Rosary as Cultural Memory

In many Cajun families, the French rosary is the last living link to the ancestral language. All Saints Day often becomes the one time of year when this prayer is spoken aloud – preserving both faith and heritage.

Catholic Teaching on Honoring the Dead

The customs of All Saints and All Souls' Day are deeply aligned with Catholic teaching:

- Praying for the dead is a **spiritual work of mercy** (cf. **CCC 1032**).
- Visiting cemeteries expresses belief in the **Communion of Saints** (cf. **CCC 954 – 959**).
- Caring for graves reflects respect for the body, a "temple of the Holy Spirit" (cf. **1 Cor 6:19**).
- The liturgical feasts emphasize the **hope of resurrection** and the unity of the heavenly and earthly Church.

Louisiana's devotional life provides a vivid, tangible expression of these truths.

The Role of Cemetery Authorities

For Cemetery Authorities, All Saints Day requires both practical and pastoral preparation:

Practical Duties

- Clearing walkways and preparing grounds
- Opening mausoleums
- Ensuring safety for large crowds
- Coordinating traffic and parking
- Working with florists and families

Pastoral Duties

- Offering hospitality
- Assisting clergy
- Helping families locate graves
- Supporting those experiencing grief
- Maintaining dignity and reverence
- Answering questions about Catholic norms

Cemetery Authorities in Louisiana often serve as stewards of tradition, helping maintain the continuity of All Saints observances across generations.

> **PASTORAL INSIGHT**
> **The Cemetery as Classroom**
>
> Children learn the faith not only in church but also in the cemetery on All Saints Day – by hearing prayers, placing flowers, and watching clergy bless their ancestors' graves. These experiences form lifelong impressions of reverence, heritage, and hope.

Contemporary Challenges and Renewed Interest

Modern life presents challenges to maintaining historic traditions:

- Families spread across states
- Decline in the French language
- Loss of family tombs through abandonment
- Reduced knowledge of cemetery customs
- Fewer priests are available for blessings

Yet interest in All Saints observances is **increasing**, not decreasing. Many young families are rediscovering the meaning, beauty, and identity tied to these days. Catholic schools in Louisiana have revived cemetery visits and cleanings, reconnecting students with cultural heritage.

CONCLUSION

All Saints Day and All Souls Day embody the heart of Louisiana Catholic burial culture. They unite theology, family memory, and community identity in one of the most powerful living traditions of the state.

These days remind the faithful that the cemetery is not a place of sorrow alone, but a place of hope—a sacred space where life, death, and eternal destiny meet.

In the chapters that follow, we will explore how these traditions shape Catholic views on cremation, the cultural practices of Louisiana's diverse communities, and the role of Cemetery Authorities in honoring sacred ground.

CHAPTER 7

CATHOLIC VIEWS ON CREMATION

Cremation has become increasingly common throughout the United States, including in Louisiana, where cultural, economic, and practical considerations have shifted funeral practices in recent decades. Yet within the Catholic Church, cremation carries specific theological and pastoral implications rooted in centuries of tradition. Understanding what the Church teaches — and why — allows priests, Cemetery Authorities, and families to navigate cremation with clarity, reverence, and fidelity to the faith.

This chapter explores the Catholic Church's teaching on cremation, its pastoral applications, and the unique ways Louisiana's culture interacts with these norms.

A History of Burial and the Early Church's Preference

For most of its history, the Catholic Church strongly preferred the burial of the body. This preference flowed from:

- Christ's own burial in the tomb
- The Church's belief in the resurrection of the body
- Reverence for the human body as a temple of the Holy Spirit (cf. **1 Cor 6:19**)

- The desire to avoid pagan practices that used cremation as a rejection of the afterlife

Early Christian communities explicitly associated burial with participation in Christ's burial and resurrection (cf. **Rom 6:4**).

Nowhere are the Church's early burial practices better preserved than in the catacombs of Rome. In family sarcophagi, one can see the cremated remains of family members who did not believe in Christ versus those who buried their bodies in the hope of the resurrection.

The Church's traditional preference for burial still remains today (cf. **CIC 1176 §3**), even though cremation is now permitted.

CULTURAL NOTE
Louisiana's Burial Identity

Above-ground tombs, family vaults, and multi-generational burial plots reflect Louisiana's deep-rooted preference for the interment of the body. Even as cremation grows, many families still choose to inter the ashes in family tombs—honoring tradition while adapting to modern practice.

The Church Permits Cremation

In 1963, the Vatican lifted its prohibition against cremation, provided the choice was not made as a denial of Christian teaching on resurrection. This permission was incorporated into the **1983 Code of Canon Law** and the **Order of Christian Funerals**.

The Church teaches:

- Cremation is allowed unless chosen for reasons contrary to the faith (cf. **CIC 1176 §3**).
- The Church prefers the body present for the Funeral Mass.
- If cremation occurs first, the ashes must still be treated with dignity.

The Church's approach is pastoral, aiming to accompany families while preserving doctrinal truths.

Why the Church Prefers Burial of the Body

The preference for burial is rooted in theology, not sentiment:

1. **Imitation of Christ**
   Jesus was buried. The faithful participate in this mystery.
2. **Respect for the body**
   The body is not disposable; it is an essential part of the person.
3. **Symbolism of burial**
   Burial expresses the resting of the body in hope of resurrection (cf. **1 Cor 15:42 – 44**).
4. **Communal identity**
   Burial grounds become places of memory, pilgrimage, prayer, and family identity.

For these reasons, burial remains the normative practice — even while cremation is allowed.

PASTORAL INSIGHT
Language Matters

Families grieving loved ones often need gentle, clear teaching. Rather than saying "the Church dislikes cremation," it is better to say:

"The Church allows cremation but prefers the body present for the funeral because of what the body means in our faith."

The Funeral Rites and Cremation

The Church strongly encourages **the presence of the body at the Funeral Mass** before cremation (cf. **OCF 413)**. This better expresses:

- Baptismal dignity
- Reverence for the body
- Continuity with Christian tradition

However, when cremation occurs first, the Funeral Mass may still be celebrated with the cremated remains present – so long as they are properly contained.

Key Points:

- The cremated remains must be placed in a dignified vessel.
- The urn takes the place of the casket.
- A white pall is **not** placed over the urn (as the urn is not analogous to a coffin).
- The rites remain essentially the same.

The Church's Teaching on the Treatment of Cremated Remains

Catholic doctrine is unequivocal:
Cremated remains must be buried or entombed in a cemetery, columbarium, or mausoleum (cf. *Ad resurgendum cum Christo*, 2016).

The Church forbids:

- Scattering ashes on land or water
- Dividing ashes among family members
- Keeping ashes at home
- Incorporating ashes into jewelry, art, or objects
- Storing ashes indefinitely without interment

These practices undermine both the unity of the person and the hope of resurrection.

GROUND LESSONS
"We Will Scatter Them in the Bayou"

A common Louisiana pastoral dilemma arises when families request to scatter ashes in a bayou, hunting camp, or fishing ground. Although deeply meaningful to the family, this practice is **not permitted** by Catholic teaching. Cemetery Authorities and clergy must compassionately guide families toward proper interment that honors both faith and culture.

Why the Church Insists on Interment

The interment of cremated remains is required for several reasons:

- **Unity of the person:** Ashes represent the whole human body and must remain intact.
- **Public witness:** Burial in consecrated ground manifests faith in resurrection.
- **Avoiding the "disappearance" of the dead:** Keeping ashes at home often leads to neglect, loss, or accidental disposal.
- **Communal memory:** Cemeteries are places of prayer and remembrance.
- **Continuity:** Burial preserves the most fundamental Catholic instinct: the dead belong to God and the Church.

CULTURAL NOTE
Placing Ashes in Family Tombs

In Louisiana, placement of an urn inside an above-ground family tomb is very common. This practice is entirely permissible, as long as:

- The urn is secure,
- The placement is recorded,
- And the tomb remains used only as a place of final interment.

Many families appreciate cremation while maintaining multi-generational burial customs.

Cremation and Catholic Cemeteries

Catholic cemeteries in Louisiana increasingly include:

- Columbarium walls
- Free-standing columbaria
- Indoor niche chapels
- Sections within mausoleums
- Spaces within family vaults

Cremation sections are consecrated or blessed (cf. **CIC 1207**), ensuring that cremated remains receive the same dignity as bodily remains.

Administrative Considerations for Cemeteries

- Secure niche doors
- Clear labeling and recordkeeping
- Permanent memorialization
- Compliance with diocesan policy
- Ensuring reverence and uniformity in layout

Catholic cemeteries must maintain the sacred character of cremation areas, just as with traditional burial grounds.

Common Pastoral Questions

"Can we divide the ashes among family members?"

No. Ashes must remain intact (cf. *Ad resurgendum*, 6).

"Can we keep the ashes at home until we decide?"

Only temporarily and for a short, pastorally necessary time.

"Can we place the urn inside a family tomb?"

Yes — this is a longstanding practice in Louisiana.

"Can we scatter ashes on family property?"

No. Ashes must be wholly interred.

"Can ashes be buried with another body?"

Yes. Many dioceses permit placement with a spouse in the same crypt or grave.

PASTORAL INSIGHT
Explaining the Why

When families understand *why* ashes must be interred — not simply that it is "a rule" — they are far more receptive:

- It honors the person.
- It protects their memory.
- It expresses belief in resurrection.
- It ensures care by future generations.

Cremation and Louisiana Culture

Louisiana's shift toward cremation is influenced by:

- Cost considerations
- Changing family structures
- Mobility across states
- Smaller family units handling burial decisions
- Fewer family tombs are being actively maintained
- Weather challenges with traditional burial

Yet Louisiana families often blend cremation with longstanding cultural practices:

- Placing urns in family mausoleums
- Holding rosaries and vigils before cremation
- Conducting traditional All Saints' blessings over niches
- Maintaining memorial cards, photos, and French devotions

Cremation, when carried out in accordance with Catholic teaching, becomes harmonized with Louisiana's unique burial culture.

Conclusion

Catholic teaching on cremation maintains a delicate balance: **pastoral flexibility** and **theological integrity**.

The Church recognizes changing cultural realities but remains firm in safeguarding:

- The dignity of the human body
- The unity of the person
- The hope of the resurrection
- The sacredness of burial
- The communal identity of Catholic cemeteries

In Louisiana, cremation has found a respectful place within a rich tradition of family tombs, sacred ground, and communal remembrance.

The next chapter will explore the diverse **Cajun and Creole burial customs** that continue to shape Louisiana's sacred landscape.

PART III

CULTURAL BURIAL PRACTICES IN LOUISIANA

CHAPTER 8

CAJUN & CREOLE BURIAL CUSTOMS

Cajun and Creole communities have shaped Louisiana's burial culture in ways unmatched anywhere else in the United States. Their customs reflect a blend of Catholic faith, French and Spanish colonial memory, African and Afro-Caribbean influence, Native American heritage, and the lived experience of families tied deeply to land, community, and ancestry.

Cajun and Creole burial traditions bring color, sound, ritual, and reverence to the universal Catholic teaching on death and resurrection. These customs create a uniquely Louisiana expression of faith—one where the sacred and the familial meet at the graveside.

Historical Roots of Cajun & Creole Burial Practice

The Cajun Experience

The Acadians who settled in Louisiana after the 1755 expulsion from Nova Scotia (Acadie) brought with them a strong Catholic identity, family-centered living, and burial practices rooted in rural French tradition. Burials took place near parish churches or in small family plots, with simple wooden or masonry markers, rosaries prayed in French, and strong communal support.

The Creole Experience

Louisiana Creole culture – born from the blending of French, Spanish, African, Caribbean, and Native influences – carried burial traditions marked by:

- Strong Catholic devotion
- Rich musical expressions
- Ritual respect for ancestors
- Family tombs and above-ground vaults
- Community processions and public mourning

Both traditions developed in the unique landscape of South Louisiana, where high water tables, plantation life, Catholic parish centers, and blended cultures created a burial ethos unlike any other.

CULTURAL NOTE
"We Bury Our Dead Together"

Both Cajun and Creole communities historically placed enormous importance on family tombs. Burials in the family vault were not merely practical – they were a symbol of identity, continuity, and belonging to one's people.

Above-Ground Tombs and Family Vaults

In many parts of Louisiana, above-ground burial is not simply a response to geography. It is a cultural statement.

Reasons for Above-Ground Burial:

- High water table in coastal regions
- French and Spanish burial influence
- Symbolism of family unity
- Preservation of remains in masonry structures
- Local preference for visible, enduring family monuments

Family vaults, often passed down through generations, serve as both resting places and tangible records of ancestry. Many are carefully maintained, whitewashed, and decorated each year during All Saints observances.

> **GROUND LESSONS**
> **The Family Tomb as an Heirloom**
>
> For Cajun and Creole families, the tomb is often considered the most important inheritance—more meaningful than land or livestock. Families may move heaven and earth to preserve a tomb damaged by storms or neglect, because it represents the resting place of their people.

Community Mourning and Vigil Traditions

Cajun and Creole funerals historically involved strong community participation, beginning long before the funeral Mass.

Key Elements Include:

- **Extended wakes** lasting through the night, often with food, coffee, and prayers
- **French rosaries**, chanted in rhythmic cadence
- **Family storytelling** as an expression of grief and memory
- **Neighbors bringing food** – gumbo, étouffée, boudin, and other rice dishes – to support the family
- **Communal sitting with the body** in earlier generations
- **Musical expressions**, especially in Creole communities
- **Black attire or mourning veils**, especially among older Creole women

These practices expressed solidarity, faith, and mutual care – hallmarks of both cultures.

PASTORAL INSIGHT
The Wake as Evangelization

Clergy and cemetery professionals often find that the Vigil becomes a place of profound pastoral ministry. The custom of gathering long into the night opens hearts to prayer, healing, and faith conversations that might not arise elsewhere.

FUNERAL PROCESSIONS AND THE JOURNEY TO THE CEMETERY

The journey from church to cemetery holds symbolic significance for Cajun and Creole families. Historically:

- The body was carried by wagon, mule cart, or on foot.
- The community followed, praying and singing.
- Bells tolled as the procession passed through town.
- Children joined quietly, witnessing tradition firsthand.

In Creole communities — with African and Caribbean influences — funeral processions could be more rhythmic, incorporating spirituals, call-and-response chanting, or early forms of the brass processions seen later in New Orleans tradition.

Even today, slower driving from church to cemetery continues as a mark of respect.

CULTURAL NOTE
The Final Ride

In rural Cajun areas, it was common for the hearse driver to open the window and say, "This is your last ride home," as they entered the cemetery. This touching custom acknowledged both grief and faith.

Music in Cajun & Creole Funerals

Music is one of the most distinct elements of these burial traditions.

Cajun Funeral Music

- French hymns such as *"J'irai la voir un jour"*
- Slow waltzes adapted for sacred use
- Simple guitar or accordion accompaniment
- Chant-like rosary recitations in French

Creole Funeral Music

- African American spirituals
- Early jazz or brass elements
- Gospel hymns blended with Catholic repertoire
- Call-and-response singing

Music expresses both sorrow and hope, reflecting the deep emotional bonds within these communities.

GROUND LESSONS
"Singing Them Home"

In some Creole families, the phrase "We're going to sing them home" reflects the belief that music helps accompany the soul on its journey to God. This idea is not a doctrine, but a powerful cultural expression of love and faith.

THE ROLE OF FOOD AND HOSPITALITY

Food is central to Cajun and Creole mourning.

After the funeral:

- Families gather for meals, often large and communal.
- Traditional foods such as gumbo, jambalaya, red beans, or étouffée are served.
- Neighbors bring dishes to nourish the grieving.

These meals serve both practical and symbolic purposes – providing comfort, community support, and a sense of continuity amid loss.

FRENCH ROSARIES AND PRAYER TRADITIONS

French - Catholic devotion remains a hallmark of Cajun and Creole funerals:

- Rosaries are prayed in French
- French prayer cards
- French hymns are sung at the vigil and graveside
- Candles and holy cards left on tombs
- Elder family members leading communal prayer

These devotions reinforce cultural identity and connect families to ancestral Catholic practices.

CULTURAL NOTE
The Chanté Rosary

Some communities practiced the *chanté rosary*—a sung rosary with melodic call-and-response phrases, often accompanied by accordion or unaccompanied vocal harmony. This tradition remains alive in a few parishes today.

The Structure of Burial in Family Vaults

Cajun and Creole family vaults have distinctive burial patterns shaped by tradition and practicality:

- Each vault is sealed with brick or granite.
- When space is needed, remains may be respectfully removed or placed in lower ossuary chambers.
- Names are added to the front panel as generations join the tomb.
- Tombs are reopened only after the canonical norms and civil regulations for re-entry are observed.

This structure ensures continuity and keeps families physically united in death.

PASTORAL INSIGHT
Compassionate Education

When families unfamiliar with tomb burial encounter older practices – such as temporary removal of remains or the natural, rapid decomposition caused by heat – a gentle explanation is essential. Many find comfort when they understand the cultural and theological reasoning.

Mourning Practices: Black Veils, Rosaries, and Ritual Dress

Older generations of Creole women practiced **veiling** during funerals or periods of mourning, wearing black lace mantillas as signs of solemnity and respect. Cajun widows often wore black dresses for extended mourning.

Other mourning customs include:

- Placing a rosary in the hands of the deceased
- Dressing the deceased in Sunday best
- Using blessed candles during the vigil

These customs blend Catholic symbolism with regional cultural identity.

All Saints Day and the Cajun & Creole Cemetery

As explored in Chapter 6, All Saints Day is especially vibrant in Cajun and Creole communities. Customs include:

- Whitewashing family tombs
- Placing chrysanthemums and candles
- Praying French rosaries
- Participating in the blessing of the graves
- Gathering for family reunions at the cemetery

These practices reinforce identity and ensure that ancestral memory remains alive across generations.

Blended Religious Influences

Creole communities, in particular, reflect blended heritage. Catholic devotion sometimes intermingles with elements of African-based cultural ritual, including:

- Emphasis on ancestors
- Musical expressions reminiscent of West African traditions
- Symbolic items are placed at home shrines before the funeral

These expressions are cultural, not religiously syncretistic, and are generally separate from Catholic liturgical practice.

GROUND LESSONS
Pastoral Sensitivity in Blended Cultures

Occasionally, families may request rituals that are not appropriate for the Catholic liturgy (e.g., symbolic offerings at the coffin). Cemetery Authorities and clergy must explain what is permitted in the rite while affirming the cultural meaning behind the request.

Theological Consistency Within Cultural Practice

Cajun and Creole burial traditions are fully compatible with Catholic theology when practiced in the appropriate context.

These customs affirm:

- The dignity of the dead
- The hope of resurrection
- The importance of prayer
- The bond of family and community
- The reverence for sacred ground

They enrich, rather than replace, the universal Catholic rites.

Conclusion

Cajun and Creole burial customs are among the most cherished expressions of Catholic faith in Louisiana. These traditions – rooted in family, land, and devotion – create a sacred tapestry woven from centuries of experience.

They reveal a profound truth: **faith is not lived in abstraction, but in community**, in ritual, in memory, and in the ways we honor our dead.

In the next chapter, we will explore **African American burial traditions**, which further enrich Louisiana's sacred landscape with history, resilience, and spiritual depth.

CHAPTER 9

AFRICAN AMERICAN BURIAL TRADITIONS

African American burial traditions in Louisiana form one of the richest and most moving expressions of faith in the region's sacred landscape. Rooted in resilience, community, and profound spiritual conviction, these practices reflect a blend of Catholic and Protestant influences, West African cultural memory, and the lived experience of a people who transformed suffering into dignity and hope.

From the quiet rural cemeteries of Acadiana to the historic African American parishes of New Orleans, these traditions honor the dead with reverence, symbolism, and celebration, weaving together African heritage and Christian theology with remarkable beauty and depth.

Historical Foundations of African American Burial Practice

African American burial customs in Louisiana draw from multiple historical sources:

West and Central African Traditions

Enslaved Africans carried with them traditions emphasizing:

- Honoring ancestors
- Ritual respect for the dead
- Music and rhythm as expressions of grief
- Communal mourning

These elements blended organically with Louisiana's religious landscape.

Catholic and Creole Influence

Many African Americans in Louisiana were baptized in Catholic parishes dating back to the French and Spanish colonial periods. This created a unique cultural blend in which:

- Rosaries, candles, and holy water accompanied burials
- Cemeteries were consecrated spaces
- Funerals included both African and Catholic elements
- Community solidarity reinforced Catholic devotion

Segregation - Era Cemeteries

Under segregation, African Americans often established their own cemeteries, many of which remain active today. These cemeteries carry deep historical and emotional significance, serving as repositories of family legacy and cultural identity.

CULTURAL NOTE
Burial Societies

In the 19th and early 20th centuries, African American "benevolent societies" and "mutual aid societies" ensured that members received dignified funerals and burials—a profound act of charity and communal solidarity long before modern funeral insurance existed.

Community and Communal Mourning

African American funerals traditionally center around **community participation**, with large gatherings reflecting both grief and collective strength.

Common elements include:

- **Extended wakes or visitations**
- **Communal singing** (spirituals, hymns, gospel)
- **Public expressions of emotion**
- **Testimonies and remembrances**
- **Family processions** into the cemetery
- **Call-and-response prayers**

These practices weave together faith, storytelling, and shared sorrow, creating a communal experience rooted in love and resilience.

GROUND LESSONS
"Going Home"

African American funerals often use the phrase "going home," reflecting hope in eternal life and the belief that death is not an ending but a return to God. This language, drawn from both Scripture and spirituals, becomes a source of profound comfort.

Music as Prayer, Grief, and Celebration

Music plays an essential role in African American burial traditions—distinctive, emotional, and spiritually rich.

Traditional Elements Include:

- **Gospel hymns**, such as *"Swing Low, Sweet Chariot"* or *"I'll Fly Away."*
- **Spirituals**, whose lyrics express both sorrow and hope
- **Call-and-response singing** led by choirs or family members
- **A cappella mourning songs**
- **Slow, reverent hymns transitioning to celebratory music after the burial**

In historic African American Catholic parishes, this music blends seamlessly with the Funeral Mass, enriching the liturgy with cultural resonance.

CULTURAL NOTE
Jazz Funerals and African American Catholics

While often associated with New Orleans secular culture, jazz funerals have deep African American spiritual roots. Historically, many jazz funerals were conducted for Catholic African American families, blending sacred rites with musical traditions honoring both grief and resurrection.

Symbols, Grave Markers, and Decoration

African American cemeteries throughout Louisiana exhibit distinctive forms of memorialization:

Common Symbolic Practices:

- **Shells or broken pottery** placed on graves (echoing African traditions)
- **Offerings of flowers, plants, or personal items**
- **Decorative ironwork** or handmade crosses
- **Bright artificial flowers**, expressing celebration of life
- **Grave coverings** made of concrete or tile to protect gravesites
- **Home-carved or hand-painted markers**, especially in older rural cemeteries

These symbols often reflect both cultural heritage and Christian faith.

Prayer Traditions at the Graveside

African American graveside traditions emphasize emotional honesty, theological hope, and communal prayer. Common elements include:

- Scripture readings
- Prayers for the deceased's journey to heaven
- Gospel hymns were sung at the graveside
- Benedictions with uplifted hands
- A final farewell ritual (e.g., placing dirt or flowers on the casket)

In Catholic African American communities, the **Rite of Committal** is often enriched with gospel music or congregational singing, giving voice to both grief and hope.

PASTORAL INSIGHT
The Importance of Space

Cemetery Authorities must recognize that African American families may gather in large numbers, sing actively, and remain at the graveside longer than other cultural groups. Hospitality – not restriction – is the pastoral approach.

Clothing, Ritual Dress, and Cultural Expression

Distinctive attire is part of the African American mourning tradition, including:

- **Black church suits or dresses**, symbolizing respect
- **White clothing**, particularly for women, represents purity and resurrection
- **Church hats**, a cherished cultural symbol worn by women
- **Matching shirts** for family groups
- **Funeral programs** with extensive photos and tributes

Dress becomes a visible expression of dignity, tradition, and communal unity.

Processions and the Journey to Sacred Ground

African American burial traditions place strong emphasis on **the procession to the cemetery**, symbolizing:

- A shared journey of the living and the dead
- Community accompaniment
- The final act of honoring the deceased

In many Louisiana communities:

- The entire congregation follows the hearse.
- Slow, reverent travel signals respect and solidarity.
- Singing continues throughout the procession.

These practices are sacred, not merely cultural customs.

Stewardship of African American Cemeteries

Many African American cemeteries in Louisiana face significant challenges:

- Historic neglect during and after segregation
- Lack of formal records
- Weather-related damage
- Limited funds for upkeep
- Loss of local populations due to migration

Yet these cemeteries are **priceless cultural and spiritual landmarks** that hold genealogical, historical, and communal value.

Efforts throughout Louisiana now focus on preserving these sacred spaces through:

- Parish engagement
- Cultural heritage groups
- State historic preservation programs
- Community-led restoration efforts

GROUND LESSONS
The Cemetery as Archive

African American cemeteries often preserve family histories that were not recorded elsewhere due to enslavement and segregation. Tombs, markers, and burial patterns become a form of "memory archive" that carries irreplaceable cultural meaning.

African American Catholics and the Funeral Mass

African American Catholic parishes in Louisiana bring a unique richness to the Church's funeral rites:

- Gospel choirs lead liturgical music.
- Homilies emphasize both hope and the lived struggles of the deceased.
- The assembly responds vocally ("Amen," "Yes, Lord").
- The Final Commendation is often deeply emotional.
- The community participates fully in the committal rite.

These elements remain fully compatible with Catholic teaching (cf. **CIC 1176; OCF 14 – 18)**, enriching the Church's liturgy with cultural beauty.

Continuity Across Generations

African American burial traditions preserve communal identity in profound ways:

- Family tombs or plots anchor generations.
- Rituals and music pass through family lines.
- Stories shared at funerals preserve cultural memory.
- Cemeteries become places of ongoing relationship and prayer.

In Louisiana, these traditions remain vibrant because they resonate deeply with both Catholic belief and cultural history.

The Repass (Repast)

In African American funeral traditions, the **repass** (sometimes spelled *repast*) is the **gathering held after the funeral or burial service**, where family and friends come together to share a meal, offer condolences, and celebrate the life of the deceased. It serves as both a time of **communal grieving** and **healing** and is deeply rooted in cultural and spiritual traditions.

Key Features of the Repass

1. Communal Meal

- The centerpiece of the repass is a shared meal, often featuring traditional family dishes.
- In some cases, the meal is potluck-style, with extended family or church members contributing.

2. Spiritual and Emotional Support

- The repass provides emotional closure and allows for shared storytelling, prayer, gospel singing, and expressions of remembrance.
- It's common for loved ones to laugh and cry together, reflecting on the joy and sorrow of life.

3. Cultural and Historical Significance

- Historically, African American families often held repasses in homes, church fellowship halls, or community centers — especially during the era of segregation when public venues were limited.
- The repass continues to be a key cultural expression of solidarity, resilience, and reverence for ancestors.

4. Open Invitation

- Repasses are generally open to all attendees of the funeral — extended relatives, neighbors, coworkers, and church members are often welcomed.

Meaning and Purpose

The repass is more than just a meal — it's a **ritual of remembrance, resistance, and restoration.** In African American communities, where funerals are often deeply spiritual and expressive, the repass provides space for:

- **Fellowship and support** beyond the structured ceremony
- **Uplifting the legacy** of the deceased through shared memories
- **Strengthening community bonds** in the face of loss

CONCLUSION

African American burial traditions in Louisiana embody resilience, faith, and profound spiritual beauty. They reveal a community that has endured suffering, preserved dignity, and enriched Louisiana's sacred landscape with music, devotion, and ancestral memory.

These customs — shaped by African heritage, Catholic teaching, and cultural strength — offer the Church a powerful witness: **grief expressed with honesty, hope expressed with joy, and reverence expressed communally.**

CHAPTER 10

NATIVE AMERICAN BURIAL TRADITIONS

Louisiana's Native American communities possess some of the oldest continuous burial traditions in North America. Long before European arrival, the peoples of the lower Mississippi Valley honored their dead with ceremonies rooted in kinship, land, and spiritual cosmology. Today, many Native communities continue to preserve burial customs shaped by ancestral belief, Catholic influence, and the realities of modern tribal life.

Because of Louisiana's unique blend of cultures, Native American burial practices cannot be understood as a single set of traditions. Instead, they are diverse living expressions found among tribes such as the Chitimacha, Houma, Tunica-Biloxi, Coushatta, Choctaw, Caddo, and Atakapa-Ishak. These communities carry an ancient reverence for the dead—one that resonates deeply with Catholic teaching on dignity, memory, and sacred ground.

Ancient Foundations of Native Burial Practices

Archaeological evidence reveals that Native peoples of the lower Mississippi Valley practiced highly developed burial rites for thousands of years. These included:

- **Burial mounds** were used as sacred communal places
- **Grave goods** placed with the deceased
- **Ceremonial cleansing rituals**
- **Communal mourning** and gatherings
- **Earthwork structures** that oriented burials to the seasons or cardinal directions
- **Placement of bodies in specific orientations**, often symbolizing journey, renewal, or connection with the spirit world

These practices reflected a worldview in which life, death, earth, and spirit formed one interconnected whole.

CULTURAL NOTE
Mound Burial Traditions

Many tribes in the southeastern United States built earthen mounds as sacred sites, where leaders or ancestors might be interred. While these mound-building cultures were not specific to the tribes currently in Louisiana, they influenced spiritual geography throughout the region.

The Importance of Land and Ancestry

For Native American communities, land is not merely property; it is a living part of tribal identity. Burial within ancestral territory is both a spiritual and cultural imperative.

Key Beliefs Include:

- The earth receives the body with dignity.
- Burial sites maintain the bond between ancestors and future generations.
- The land carries the memory of the people.
- Displacement from ancestral burial grounds is experienced as a loss of identity and heritage.

These convictions align naturally with Catholic teachings on sacred ground and respect for the body (cf. **CCC 2300**).

GROUND LESSONS
The Pain of Displacement

Forced relocations, coastal erosion, and land loss have separated many Native families from traditional burial grounds. Some communities now work with dioceses, parishes, and preservation groups to safeguard ancestral cemeteries threatened by storms, development, and environmental change.

Catholic Influence on Native Communities

Many Native American tribes in Louisiana embraced Catholicism through the presence of French and Spanish missionaries. Catholicism blended with cultural traditions – not through syncretism but through adaptation that honored both faith and heritage.

Common Expressions Include:

- Use of holy water at burials
- Catholic funeral Masses followed by tribal ceremonies
- Rosaries said at wakes
- Crosses placed on graves
- Use of tribal textiles, baskets, or beadwork during the Vigil
- Ancestor remembrance integrated into All Saints' customs

Native Catholics often maintain a dual identity: fully Catholic and fully indigenous, weaving ancestral customs into the framework of the Church's funeral rites (cf. **CIC 1176 §§2 - 3**).

PASTORAL INSIGHT
Honor Both Traditions

Clergy and Cemetery Authorities should welcome – and encourage – tribal customs that respect Catholic teaching. For many Native Catholics, traditional rituals express reverence, not theological conflict.

Tribal Burial Customs Across Louisiana

While each tribe maintains its own unique practices, several themes appear widely:

Community Participation

Burials often involve extended family, tribal leaders, and community members. Grief is shared collectively.

Simplicity and Reverence

Many tribes value minimalism: simple graves, natural materials, and modest markers.

Grave Goods

Some families place meaningful items with the deceased (tools, baskets, beadwork). These gestures express love and belonging; they are cultural, not contrary to Catholic faith when done appropriately.

Directional Orientation

Some traditions orient graves to face the east, symbolizing dawn, renewal, or the spirit's journey—echoing ancient Christian burial orientation.

Tribal Songs and Chants

Traditional songs may accompany a burial, expressing prayer, release, and ancestral connection.

Earth and Nature Elements

Sprinkling handfuls of earth, cedar, or blessed water on the grave is common. The earth itself is a sacred witness.

These customs harmonize naturally with Catholic belief in the resurrection of the body and the dignity of the human person.

CULTURAL NOTE
Chitimacha Traditions

The Chitimacha Tribe of Louisiana historically placed family and clan identity at the center of burial practice. While modern Chitimacha Catholics participate fully in Church rites, ancestral customs – such as community gatherings and the use of traditional art–remain integral.

Mourning, Memory, and Family Identity

Native American mourning can be deeply communal, involving:

- Periods of silence and reflection
- Communal meals
- Storytelling about the deceased
- Acts of remembrance marking seasonal changes
- Visiting the grave periodically as part of the healing journey

These practices mirror Catholic traditions of praying for the dead, celebrating memorial Masses, and visiting the cemetery, especially on All Souls Day.

GROUND LESSONS
Story as a Means of Memory

In many Native cultures, storytelling at the graveside is more than reminiscence – it is a sacred act that places the deceased's life within the unbroken story of the tribe.

CEMETERY DESIGN AND SYMBOLISM

Native American cemeteries in Louisiana often feature distinctive elements:

- **Wooden or hand-carved crosses**
- **Grassy, natural landscapes**
- **Shells, beads, or meaningful objects**
- **Cedar branches or plant life** representing purification
- **Grave houses or shelters**, seen in older cemeteries
- **Tribal flags** for veterans
- **Color symbolism** tied to direction or clan identity

The aesthetic differs from the symmetrical rows of many Catholic or municipal cemeteries, emphasizing the organic, familial, and spiritual connection to the land.

The Catholic Liturgy and Tribal Cultural Expression

Native American Catholics often incorporate traditional elements **before or after** the Church's official rites:

Compatible Cultural Practices Include:

- Smudging or cleansing ceremony **outside** the liturgical rite
- Traditional drumming or singing **before or after** the Funeral Mass
- Tribal elders offering words at the Vigil
- Placing culturally significant items inside or on the coffin
- Community meals following the burial

These are expressions of heritage and identity, not competition with Catholic teaching.

PASTORAL INSIGHT
Respecting Cultural Space

Clergy and cemetery professionals need to understand which elements belong within the liturgy and which belong before or after. When boundaries are clear, cultural richness strengthens rather than conflicts with the Church's rites.

The Impact of Environmental Change on Burial Traditions

Native communities in Louisiana face significant challenges:

- Coastal land loss
- Saltwater intrusion
- Storm damage
- River migration
- Erosion affecting unmarked burial grounds

Some tribes now work with church parishes, local governments, and historians to identify, protect, and, when necessary, relocate ancestral graves in ways consistent with both tribal tradition and Catholic teaching (cf. **CIC 1212**; **La. R.S. 8:304 - 306**).

CULTURAL NOTE
Protecting the Ancestors

For many tribes, safeguarding ancestral graves is an act of sovereignty, cultural preservation, and spiritual responsibility. The cemetery is not just a place; it is part of the tribe's identity.

Native American Veterans and Honor Rituals

Native communities have a long history of military service. Burial rituals for veterans often include:

- Tribal flags
- Eagle feathers
- Veteran honor guards
- Special prayers for warriors
- Communal gatherings celebrating bravery and service

In Catholic funerals, these expressions accompany the U.S. military honors, blending patriotism, faith, and tribal identity.

Continuity and the Future of Native Burial Traditions

Despite historical injustices and environmental challenges, Native burial traditions in Louisiana remain vibrant. Young tribal members increasingly seek to preserve:

- Ancestral customs
- Tribal cemeteries
- Oral histories
- Traditional crafts related to funerary practice
- Cultural rites that accompany Catholic liturgy

This renewed interest ensures that traditional Native burial practices will continue to enrich Louisiana's cultural and Catholic landscape.

Conclusion

Native American burial traditions in Louisiana form a sacred inheritance—one that reflects centuries of reverence for the dead, intimacy with the land, and continuity across generations.

These customs harmonize beautifully with Catholic theology, expressing shared beliefs in dignity, memory, and the sacredness of burial.

In the chapters ahead, we will explore additional religious and cultural communities that contribute to Louisiana's rich tapestry of burial practices, beginning with Jewish, Protestant, and other faith traditions.

CHAPTER II

JEWISH, PROTESTANT, AND OTHER TRADITIONS

Louisiana's burial landscape reflects extraordinary religious diversity. While Catholicism has shaped much of the state's culture, Jewish, Protestant, Orthodox Christian, Muslim, and other religious communities have also contributed profoundly to the ways families honor their dead.

Understanding these traditions enables Cemetery Authorities, clergy, and pastoral workers to serve all families with respect, cultural sensitivity, and an appreciation for the sacred practices of neighboring faiths. Though each tradition differs in theology and ritual, the desire to provide dignity in death and hope for the next life unites them across belief systems.

JEWISH BURIAL TRADITIONS IN LOUISIANA

Jewish communities in Louisiana – found in New Orleans, Baton Rouge, Shreveport, Alexandria, Lafayette, and smaller cities – maintain burial customs rooted in thousands of years of tradition.

KEY JEWISH PRINCIPLES:

1. **Immediate Burial**
   Jewish law (Halakha) encourages burial as soon as possible, ideally within 24 hours (cf. **Deut 21:23**).
2. **Simplicity**
   The body is washed in a ritual called *taharah* and dressed in simple white shrouds (*tachrichim*). A plain wooden casket is used, reflecting equality before God.
3. **No Embalming, Viewing, or Cremation**
   Embalming and public viewing are generally avoided, and cremation is traditionally prohibited because the body is seen as God's creation.
4. **Graveside Service and Prayers**
   The *El Malei Rachamim* prayer and the Mourner's Kaddish express trust in God's mercy.
5. **The Dignity of the Body**
   The body is treated with profound respect, and ritual guardians (*shomerim*) may stay with it until burial.
6. **Sitting Shiva**
   After burial, families gather for a week of mourning, prayer, and community support.

CULTURAL NOTE
New Orleans' Historic Jewish Cemeteries

Some of Louisiana's oldest Jewish cemeteries date to the 1820s and feature distinctive above-ground tombs. These cemeteries document the long history of Jewish life in the state and often coexist near Catholic or Protestant burial grounds.

PROTESTANT BURIAL TRADITIONS

Protestant traditions in Louisiana are diverse, reflecting denominational, regional, and cultural distinctions. While theological emphases differ from Catholic doctrine, Protestant families share a deep reverence for Scripture, prayer, and communal mourning.

KEY FEATURES ACROSS PROTESTANT TRADITIONS:

1. **Celebration of Life Services**
   Services focus on the deceased's personal faith and the promise of eternal life in Christ. Scripture reading and preaching play central roles.
2. **Flexibility in Ritual**
   Unlike Catholic liturgy, Protestant funeral services vary widely, adapted to community tradition and pastoral preference.
3. **Music and Hymns**
   Hymns such as *"Amazing Grace," "Just a Closer Walk with Thee,"* and *"How Great Thou Art"* are deeply rooted in Louisiana culture.
4. **Cremation Accepted**
   Most Protestant communities permit cremation without theological objection.
5. **Graveside Services**
   Graveside prayers, Scripture reading, and hymn singing often accompany interment.
6. **Communal Meals**
   Funeral meals—especially in rural Baptist and Methodist communities—serve as essential pastoral and familial support.

GROUND LESSONS
The Protestant Emphasis on Testimony

In many Protestant funerals, personal testimonies about the deceased's faith journey form the heart of the service. For Catholic cemetery professionals, understanding this emphasis is crucial when assisting Protestant families.

Baptist Traditions

Baptist communities are widespread throughout Louisiana. Their funerals typically include:

- Scripture-centered preaching
- Congregational hymn singing
- Emphasis on salvation and personal faith
- Occasional altar calls or evangelistic moments
- Community meals following the burial

Burial practices are straightforward, reflecting Baptist values of humility and biblical focus.

Methodist Traditions

Methodist funerals combine Scripture, liturgy, and community support. Common practices include:

- Use of the *United Methodist Book of Worship*
- Pastoral prayers emphasizing grace
- Memorial hymns
- Flexibility in cremation or burial

Methodists often emphasize God's presence in suffering and the promise of eternal life.

Pentecostal and Charismatic Traditions

Pentecostal funerals are deeply emotional and expressive:

- Vibrant music – choirs, gospel groups, praise songs
- Spontaneous prayers and testimonies
- A celebration of the deceased's spiritual journey
- Extended services that reflect the community's warmth and solidarity

These services blend grief and joy, affirming the deceased's entrance into eternal life.

PASTORAL INSIGHT
Accommodating Longer Services

Pentecostal and Charismatic funerals can be significantly longer than Catholic or mainline Protestant services. Cemetery Authorities should expect extended graveside gatherings, music, and prayer – and offer respectful flexibility.

Orthodox Christian Traditions

Orthodox Christian communities — Greek, Antiochian, Ethiopian, and Russian — are found primarily in metropolitan Louisiana.

Distinctive Elements Include:

- Prayers for the repose of the soul
- Use of incense, icons, and chanting
- Traditional prohibition of cremation
- Burial of the body after a Divine Liturgy or Funeral Service
- Forty-day memorial prayers
- Highly symbolic vestments and rituals

Orthodox cemeteries may have distinctive iconography and cross forms.

Muslim Burial Traditions in Louisiana

Muslim communities in Louisiana continue long-standing Islamic burial practices:

Core Elements:

- Burial as soon as possible after death
- Washing and shrouding the body (*ghusl* and *kafan*)
- No embalming or cremation
- Simple grave, typically with the body facing Mecca
- Graveside prayer (*Salat al-Janazah*)
- Avoidance of elaborate decoration

Islamic cemeteries or dedicated Muslim sections are increasingly present in urban Louisiana.

> **CULTURAL NOTE**
> **Shared Values with Catholic Teaching**
>
> Many Islamic burial values – simplicity, bodily dignity, prompt burial – mirror Catholic principles, fostering natural mutual respect among cemetery professionals.

Hindu, Buddhist, and Other Traditions

Smaller but growing Hindu and Buddhist communities also influence Louisiana's burial landscape:

Hindu Practices:

- Preference for cremation
- Ritual purification and offerings
- Scattering of ashes (though this can create challenges when using Catholic cemeteries)

Buddhist Practices:

- Chanting and meditation ceremonies
- Cremation is a common practice
- Use of incense and ritual offerings

Cemetery Authorities must navigate these practices sensitively, especially where Catholic norms prohibit scattering or the use of certain ritual objects.

Interfaith Considerations for Cemetery Authorities

Cemetery professionals in Louisiana often serve families from various religious backgrounds. Essential considerations include:

- Respecting religious requirements for burial timing
- Understanding views on cremation
- Accommodating prayer services and processions
- Clarifying cemetery policies without diminishing cultural expression
- Navigating interfaith families, especially those blending Catholic and Protestant elements
- Maintaining the dignity of sacred ground across traditions

PASTORAL INSIGHT
"Sacred for All, Catholic in Identity"

Catholic cemeteries welcome people of many traditions, especially relatives of Catholics. The cemetery's *identity* remains Catholic, but its *hospitality* embraces all who seek a dignified burial.

CONCLUSION

Jewish, Protestant, Orthodox, Muslim, and other faith traditions contribute profoundly to Louisiana's diverse burial landscape. Each tradition brings its own rituals, theology, and cultural expressions—but all reflect a shared human longing for dignity, remembrance, community, and hope in the face of death.

Understanding these traditions allows Cemetery Authorities and Catholic leaders to minister with respect, pastoral sensitivity, and cultural awareness.
Together, they form a tapestry of sacred practices that enrich Louisiana's identity as a place where the dead are honored, and the living are supported with compassion.

PART IV

SEASONAL, ICONIC, AND LOCAL TRADITIONS

CHAPTER 12

GRAVESIDE SYMBOLS AND ICONOGRAPHY

Cemeteries are not only places of rest — they are visual catechisms. Every symbol carved in stone, every statue placed atop a tomb, every decorative motif recalls a story of faith, hope, culture, or family identity. In Louisiana, these symbols form a language spoken across generations, weaving together Catholic theology, French and Spanish colonial influence, African and Caribbean spirituality, Native tradition, and the intimate history of the families who shaped the land.

This chapter explores the meanings of the symbols, imagery, and iconography commonly found in Louisiana cemeteries, revealing how graveside art serves as a testament to belief, heritage, and sacred memory.

The Cemetery as a Theology in Stone

Christian iconography has long used visual symbols to communicate eternal truths—especially in places of burial. Sacred art at gravesites conveys:

- Belief in the Resurrection
- Hope in Christ
- Devotion to the saints
- The dignity of the human person
- Family continuity
- Cultural identity

Symbols become a silent homily—expressing what words cannot.

In Louisiana, where cemeteries often sit at the center of communal life, these visual elements serve as landmarks of faith and culture.

CULTURAL NOTE
Art Formed by Climate and Materials

Louisiana's cemeteries contain unique iconography shaped by:

- High humidity and heat
- Abundance of local brick and stucco
- French and Spanish tomb architecture
- A tradition of hand-crafted religious art
- Local Catholic devotional objects

This blend produces an aesthetic found nowhere else.

The Cross: The Central Symbol of Christian Burial

The cross is the most universal Christian symbol and appears in countless forms across Louisiana cemeteries.

Common Types of Crosses:

- **Latin Cross** – the standard symbol of Christian burial.
- **Greek Cross** – equal arms, often used in older tombs.
- **Crucifix** – depicts Christ's Body, emphasizing sacrifice and redemption.
- **Celtic Cross** – common in areas with Irish influence.
- **Flared or fleur-de-lis crosses** – blending French heritage with Christian symbolism.
- **Cross-in-relief** on mausoleum doors or vault facades.

Symbolic Meaning:

- Victory over death (cf. **1 Cor 15:55**)
- Identity as a follower of Christ
- Baptismal union with Christ's death and resurrection
- A reminder of eternal hope

GROUND LESSONS
The Cross as Family Identity

Some Cajun and Creole families design unique family crosses that blend cultural motifs with traditional Christian imagery. These crosses can become intergenerational symbols passed down for use in funerary design.

The Fleur-de-Lis and French Catholic Identity

The **fleur-de-lis**—a stylized lily—appears on countless Louisiana headstones, tombs, and mausoleums.

Meanings Include:

- Purity associated with the Blessed Virgin Mary
- French heritage and Acadian identity
- A symbol of Louisiana pride
- Royal dignity, tied to the Catholic monarchical tradition

Its widespread use symbolizes both Catholic devotion and local identity.

Angels: Messengers, Guardians, and Symbols of Hope

Angels are among the most beloved cemetery symbols.

Common Angel Depictions:

- **Guardian angels** are watching over the tomb
- **Weeping angels**, mourning with the living
- **Trumpeting angels**, announcing the resurrection
- **Childlike cherubs**, representing innocence or the death of a child

Theological Significance:

- Messengers of God (cf. **CCC 328 - 336**)
- Guides for the soul into heaven
- Witnesses to the Resurrection
- Symbols of comfort and protection

In Louisiana, angel statues often show weathered patina, giving them a hauntingly beautiful appearance.

> **CULTURAL NOTE**
> **Angels in Creole Art**
>
> In Creole Catholic communities, angels sometimes appear in bright colors or folk-inspired designs, blending Catholic belief with African and Caribbean artistic traditions.

The Sacred Heart of Jesus and the Immaculate Heart of Mary

These two devotions appear frequently on tombs, especially in Catholic sections:

Sacred Heart of Jesus

- Symbolizes Christ's mercy and love
- Often depicted in relief sculptures on vault doors

Immaculate Heart of Mary

- Symbol of maternal intercession
- Associated with hope, sorrow, and tenderness

These symbols express trust in God's mercy and Mary's care for the deceased.

STATUES OF SAINTS AND THEIR MEANINGS

Louisiana cemeteries often include statues of saints whose lives reflect family identity or local devotion.

COMMON SAINTS INCLUDE:

- **St. Joseph** – patron of a happy death
- **St. Francis of Assisi** – symbol of peace and humility
- **St. Anthony of Padua** – popular in Italian and Creole communities
- **St. Jude** – invoked in times of difficulty
- **St. Michael the Archangel** – protector of souls
- **St. Thérèse of Lisieux** – beloved among Cajun Catholics

SYMBOLIC FUNCTIONS:

- Emblems of intercession
- Cultural markers
- Visual testimonies of the family's devotion

These statues often bear signs of age and devotion—flowers, rosaries, or candles placed by loved ones.

PASTORAL INSIGHT
Respecting Devotional Art

Cemetery Authorities should treat graveside statues with care. Many families view these objects as part of their loved ones' spiritual identity, not mere decoration. If the rules do not permit these, explain this to families and try to find an amicable solution.

ROSARIES, PRAYER BEADS, AND DEVOTIONAL OBJECTS

Rosaries often adorn headstones or are placed inside mausoleum crypts. While exposed rosaries may degrade in Louisiana's climate, families continue this practice as a symbol of:

- Prayer for the deceased
- Marian devotion
- Continuity of Catholic faith
- Familial identity

Other devotional items found near graves include:

- Holy cards
- Scapulars
- Medals
- Blessed candles
- Crucifixes
- Small memorial plaques

These objects create a portable shrine that extends the funeral rites into ongoing remembrance.

Symbols of Death and Resurrection

Christian iconography often includes symbolic forms associated with both mortality and resurrection.

Common Symbols:

- **Alpha and Omega** – Christ as beginning and end (cf. Rev 22:13)
- **Chi-Rho (XP)** – ancient monogram of Christ
- **Doves** – peace, Holy Spirit, the soul's ascent to God
- **Lamb** – Christ, especially for children's graves
- **Palm branches** – victory over death
- **Sunrise motifs** – resurrection and new life
- **Open Gates** – entrance to heaven
- **Wheat and grape motifs** – Eucharistic symbolism of eternal life

These symbols are especially common on older tombs and in Catholic cemeteries.

CULTURAL NOTE
Resurrection Symbols in Cajun Art

In Cajun communities, hand-painted sunrise or dove motifs may appear on vaults, reflecting folk art traditions blended with Catholic belief.

Personalized Iconography: Family Stories in Stone

Many Louisiana tombs display personalized symbols that speak to the individual's life:

- **Fishing nets, boats, or shrimp trawls** – common in coastal parishes
- **Musical instruments** – honoring Cajun, Zydeco, or Creole musicians
- **Military emblems** – service branches, medals, or unit insignia
- **Occupational symbols** – carpentry tools, farming implements
- **Fraternal organizations** – Knights of Columbus, Masons (in non-Catholic contexts)
- **Tribal motifs** – in Native American Catholic cemeteries

These symbols honor vocation, heritage, and personal identity.

GROUND LESSONS
When Personal Symbolism Conflicts with Cemetery Rules

Families occasionally request symbols or imagery that are not appropriate for a Catholic cemetery (e.g., secular memorial statues, culturally sensitive items, or non-Christian religious icons). Cemetery Authorities must balance pastoral sensitivity with fidelity to the cemetery's Catholic identity.

Symbolism in Tomb Architecture

The architecture of Louisiana tombs carries symbolic meaning:

Vault Shapes

- **Gabled roofs** – echo church architecture
- **Arched niches** – symbolize heaven
- **Rounded tops** – signify eternity
- **Stepped tombs** – reminiscent of ancient mound structures

Material Choices

- Marble – purity, dignity
- Brick and stucco – strength and permanence
- Cast iron – southern craftsmanship
- Granite – endurance

Decorative Elements

- Fleur-de-lis carvings
- Iron cross finials
- French inscriptions
- Artistic relief panels

Tombs serve as monuments not only to individuals but also to families, culture, and communal identity.

Inscriptions and Epitaphs

Louisiana epitaphs often reveal linguistic and cultural diversity:

- **French inscriptions** ("Ici repose...")
- **Creole patois phrases**
- **Biblical verses**
- **Rosary or Marian invocations**
- **Nicknames reflecting local culture**

Epitaphs may express:

- Hope ("He rests with the Lord")
- Grief ("Our beloved mother")
- Identity ("A proud Creole")
- Faith ("Pray for his soul")

These inscriptions serve as miniature biographies etched in stone.

Conclusion

Graveside symbols and iconography transform Louisiana cemeteries into sacred galleries of faith and culture. Through crosses, angels, saints, inscriptions, and personal motifs, families proclaim their beliefs, honor their heritage, and express enduring love for the deceased.

These symbols remind us that cemeteries are not places of forgetting—they are places of storytelling. In Louisiana, the story is rich, layered, and profoundly Catholic, yet deeply shaped by the diverse cultures that make this region unique.

The next chapter will explore **Decoration Traditions and Cemetery Conduct**, where cultural customs intersect with pastoral care and cemetery stewardship.

CHAPTER 13

DECORATION TRADITIONS AND CEMETERY CONDUCT

Cemeteries in Louisiana are not silent fields of stone – they are vibrant places of devotion, memory, and cultural expression. Decorations placed on graves reflect love, grief, and the desire to honor family heritage. In Cajun, Creole, African American, Native American, and Catholic communities, grave decoration carries symbolic weight, transforming the cemetery into a living testament of identity and prayer.

Yet decorations must also respect the sacred nature of Catholic cemeteries and the practical responsibility of Cemetery Authorities to maintain order, safety, and reverence. This chapter explores Louisiana's diverse decoration traditions and outlines principles of conduct that preserve dignity while honoring culture.

THE PURPOSE OF GRAVESIDE DECORATION

Decorating a loved one's grave expresses several meaningful values:

- **Love and remembrance**
- **Connection to ancestors**
- **Cultural identity**
- **Hope in the Resurrection** (cf. **CCC 1681 - 1690**)

- **Devotion to the saints and the Blessed Virgin Mary**
- **Continuity across generations**

Families decorate graves because memory is sacred. Louisiana communities, in particular, hold deep reverence for family tombs, often maintaining them with care passed down from grandparents to grandchildren.

> **CULTURAL NOTE**
> **The Cemetery as Family Space**
>
> In many Louisiana parishes, the cemetery is visited as frequently as a family home. Families bring children to learn their heritage, place flowers on anniversaries, and pray the rosary during visits. Decoration becomes a form of catechesis and cultural continuity.

Types of Decorations Common in Louisiana Cemeteries

Louisiana's cemeteries display a colorful spectrum of decorations, often reflecting local culture, faith, and seasons.

Flowers

- **Fresh flowers** – associated with life and resurrection
- **Artificial flowers** – resilient in Louisiana weather
- **Chrysanthemums** – especially used on All Saints' Day
- **Roses** – devotion to Mary and the saints

Religious Items

- Rosaries
- Crucifixes
- Saint medals or statues
- Prayer cards
- Blessed candles (where permitted)

Cultural Symbols

- Fleur-de-lis
- Flags representing nationality, tribe, or community
- Religious mottos in French or Creole
- Folk-art objects

Seasonal Decorations

- All Saints Day displays
- Christmas wreaths
- Easter lilies
- Memorial Day flags for veterans

Personal Items

These may include:

- Image of fishing gear for coastal families
- Musical symbols for Cajun or Creole musicians
- Family photos
- Hobbies represented in small tokens
- Military or fraternal emblems

When done reverently, these items celebrate the fullness of a person's life.

GROUND LESSONS
When Personal Items Become Problematic

Stuffed animals, balloons, solar lights, wind chimes, or fragile objects often do not withstand Louisiana's weather. These can:

- Blow away during storms
- Interfere with lawn equipment
- Create safety hazards
- Accumulate as debris

Cemetery Authorities must balance compassion with maintenance needs.

The Role of All Saints Day Decorations

As explored in Chapter 6, All Saints' Day remains the most important day for cemetery decoration in Louisiana.

Common customs include:

- Whitewashing tombs
- Placing chrysanthemums or fresh flowers
- Cleaning and clearing old decorations
- Setting candles or lanterns
- Placing rosaries and prayer cards

These decorations are both devotional and cultural, marking the cemetery as a place where heaven and earth meet.

Catholic Teaching on Decoration and Reverence

Catholic cemeteries are sacred places (cf. **CIC 1205 - 1210**). Decorations should reflect:

- Prayerful remembrance
- Dignity
- Respect for the dead
- Harmony with the cemetery's sacred identity

Overly secular or non-Christian symbols may conflict with the cemetery's Catholic character and require guidance from Cemetery Authorities.

Permitted Symbols Generally Include:

- Crosses
- Crucifixes
- Rosaries
- Catholic devotions
- Family-appropriate personal items
- Flowers

Restricted or Prohibited Symbols Often Include:

- Non-Christian religious icons
- Occult or superstitious objects
- Offensive or inappropriate imagery
- Decorations that interfere with liturgical rites

PASTORAL INSIGHT
"Explain, Don't Just Enforce"

Families mourning a loved one often act out of affection, not with the intention to break rules. Cemetery Authorities should frame policies in terms of:

- Reverence
- Safety
- Uniformity
- Respect for all families

Clarity delivered with compassion prevents conflict.

Managing Decorations: Parish and Cemetery Policies

Cemetery policies vary, but typically address:

Placement

- On the headstone or in designated vases
- Avoiding walkways, lawn equipment areas, or adjoining plots

Duration

- Seasonal items are removed after specific dates
- Flowers are refreshed or removed when they deteriorate

Safety

- No glass vases (risk of shattering)
- No open flames except in controlled All Saints ceremonies
- No unstable items that may fall or blow away

Maintenance

- Decorations must not impede mowing or cleaning
- Prohibited items are removed periodically
- Families encouraged to check decorations after storms

Uniformity in Mausoleums

- Decorations must not block other crypts
- Adhesives or tape on marble are typically prohibited
- Flowers placed in approved vases only

> **CULTURAL NOTE**
> **Managing Expectations in a Multi-Cultural Cemetery**
>
> In Louisiana's culturally diverse cemeteries, families may have strong expectations shaped by cultural burial heritage. Policies should be clear, communicated in advance, and explained as stewardship—not restriction.

Photos, Portraits, and Porcelain Images

Cemetery Authorities frequently encounter issues with grave photos:

Permitted (in most Catholic cemeteries):

- **Porcelain portraits**, professionally adhered and weather-safe
- Embedded ceramic or enamel images
- Portraits placed *inside* mausoleum crypts

Not Permitted:

- Photos with **glass fronts**
- Frames with **cardboard backing**
- Items taped, glued, or strapped to crypt doors
- Laminated photos are not rated for outdoor use

These restrictions protect:

- Safety
- Aesthetics
- Uniformity
- Long-term preservation

GROUND LESSONS
"Glass and Wind Don't Mix"

Louisiana cemeteries regularly experience high winds and thunderstorms. Glass-fronted portraits fall, shatter, and scatter shards across walkways—creating dangerous conditions for visitors and staff. Thus, most cemeteries remove such items immediately for safety.

Conduct in Catholic Cemeteries

Catholic cemeteries are places of prayer and reverence. Conduct guidelines help maintain this sacred atmosphere.

Expected Conduct:

- Speaking softly
- Respecting other visitors
- Appropriate dress
- Keeping children supervised
- Observing quiet during committal rites
- Respecting all graves, not just one's own

Prohibited Conduct:

- Loud or disruptive behavior
- Playing loud music
- Littering
- Climbing on or leaning heavily on tombs
- Walking directly on graves unless necessary
- Entering mausoleums without permission
- Alcohol consumption (except permitted cultural events, e.g., certain second-line traditions—but even these must respect cemetery policy)

PASTORAL INSIGHT
Balancing Grief and Reverence

Families in deep grief may unintentionally break norms. Leading with compassion while gently guiding expectations upholds the dignity of the space.

Poorly Maintained or Neglected Decorations

Over time, decorations degrade. Cemetery staff must:

- Remove weather-damaged items
- Clear debris
- Restore visual harmony
- Avoid allowing clutter that diminishes dignity
- Ensure safety for visitors

This is not "erasing memory," but preserving the sacred environment.

Cultural Expressions to Honor and Preserve

Cemetery Authorities should affirm cultural expressions that:

- Respect Catholic teaching
- Are safe and durable
- Do not impede maintenance
- Contribute to the cemetery's spiritual atmosphere

This includes:

- French rosaries
- Creole devotional items
- Native American prayer objects are placed appropriately
- African American memorial ribbons or wreaths
- Military flags
- Veterans' honors
- Unique cultural symbols are used respectfully

Louisiana cemeteries thrive when culture and reverence work together.

CONCLUSION

Decoration traditions in Louisiana cemeteries reveal a rich tapestry of faith, family love, and cultural identity. When guided by reverence, safety, and Catholic values, these traditions enhance the sacred beauty of burial grounds.

Proper conduct and thoughtful regulation ensure that cemeteries remain places of dignity, memory, and spiritual peace—spaces where the living honor their dead with devotion, and where culture finds expression in harmony with the Church's mission.

The next chapter will explore **Louisiana's Musical Funerals**, bringing together one of the state's most iconic cultural practices with Catholic burial traditions.

CHAPTER 14

LOUISIANA'S MUSICAL FUNERALS

No aspect of Louisiana burial culture is more iconic, more studied, or more emotionally powerful than its musical funerals. From the slow, mournful hymns of Cajun and Creole processions to the soul-stirring, brass-led second lines of New Orleans, music transforms burial rites into a deeply expressive act of communal mourning and theological hope.

These traditions reveal not only cultural richness but also the profound connection between the human experience of grief and the Christian proclamation of resurrection. In Louisiana, music becomes prayer. Music becomes lament. Music becomes memory. And ultimately, music becomes hope.

ORIGINS OF MUSICAL FUNERALS IN LOUISIANA

Louisiana's musical funeral traditions arise from a convergence of cultural influences:

African Traditions

West and Central African cultures used:

- Drumming
- Call-and-response singing
- Communal lament
- Celebratory music to honor the dead

These customs were carried into Louisiana through enslaved people who maintained musical memory under oppression.

Catholic and Creole Influence

French and Spanish Catholic practices reinforced:

- Processions accompanied by chant
- Liturgical hymns at funerals
- Community participation at the graveside

The blending of African rhythmic tradition with Catholic ritual structure produced something uniquely Louisiana.

Jazz and Brass Band Development

By the late 19th century:

- Brass bands became central to African American social life in New Orleans.
- Benevolent societies funded funerals and hired musicians.
- Music accompanied the deceased from home to church to cemetery.

Over time, this evolved into the world-famous **jazz funeral**.

CULTURAL NOTE
Benevolent Societies and "Social Aid and Pleasure Clubs"

These clubs provided:

- Burial insurance
- Band participation
- Communal support
- Processional leadership

They were essential for African American dignity in eras of discrimination.

The Structure of a Louisiana Musical Funeral

A traditional musical funeral typically features two contrasting musical movements:

The "Dirge" Phase – Mourning

This portion includes:

- Slow, somber hymns
- Minor-key brass arrangements
- Spirituals such as *"Nearer My God to Thee"*
- Mournful drumming patterns

It accompanies:

- The funeral procession from the church
- The walk to the cemetery
- The burial itself

It reflects the reality of grief and loss.

The "Celebration" Phase – Hope

After the burial or final commendation:

- Music shifts to lively rhythms
- Brass bands launch into upbeat songs
- Participants dance, clap, and celebrate

This symbolizes:

- Victory of life over death
- The soul's entrance into eternal joy
- Communal resilience

This celebratory phase is sometimes called the **second line**.

GROUND LESSONS
The Second Line Is Not a Mardi Gras Parade

Despite tourist misconceptions, a traditional second line is not entertainment. It is a sacred cultural expression of **hope after grief**, deeply rooted in African American spirituality and Catholic belief in eternal life.

Catholic Funeral Rites and Musical Traditions

While traditional jazz or brass music is **not** used inside the Funeral Mass (cf. OCF norms), Louisiana families often integrate musical traditions:

- **Before Mass** – solemn brass hymns or organ/gospel arrangements
- **After Mass** – slow dirge outside the church
- **Procession to the cemetery** – brass band leads
- **At the cemetery**, quiet hymns or spirituals accompany the committal
- **After the burial**, the celebratory second line begins

These practices are fully compatible with Catholic teaching when used appropriately outside the liturgy (cf. **CIC 1176; OCF 14–18**).

PASTORAL INSIGHT
"Honor Culture Without Altering the Sacred"

Clergy and Cemetery Authorities can embrace Louisiana's musical heritage by guiding families to include musical elements **before or after** official rites—maintaining the reverence of the liturgy while celebrating culture.

Music in Cajun and Creole Funerals

Outside New Orleans, Cajun and Creole communities maintain their own musical funeral customs:

Cajun Funerals

- French hymns are sung at wakes or gravesides
- Accordion or fiddle accompanying family prayer
- Slow, waltz-like melodies expressing grief

Creole Funerals (Outside New Orleans)

- Gospel choirs singing at the graveside
- Call-and-response spirituals
- French-Creole hymns

These traditions emphasize:

- Family unity
- Hope in resurrection
- Cultural continuity

Though less publicized than jazz funerals, they are just as deeply woven into Louisiana's spiritual life.

The Theology Behind Musical Funerals

Musical funerals express several theological truths:

Grief Is Real

The slow, mournful opening of a jazz funeral recognizes the sorrow of loss.

Hope Is Certain

The joyous second line proclaims Christ's victory over death (cf. 1 Cor 15:54–55).

Heaven Is Celebration

The lively music symbolizes the soul entering eternal joy.

Death Is Transformation

Music reflects the Catholic belief that death changes life, not ends it (cf. Preface I of Christian Death).

Community Is Essential

Musical funerals show that mourning is not private—it is a communal act.

CULTURAL NOTE
"Cutting the Body Loose"

In some African American traditions, the moment the second line begins is called "cutting the body loose" – symbolizing both releasing the soul to God and releasing the community from mourning.

The Role of Brass Bands and Musicians

Musicians at Louisiana funerals carry a sacred responsibility. Their presence:

- Honors cultural identity
- Accompanies the deceased on their final journey
- Supports the grieving
- Bears witness to Catholic hope

Many musicians consider funeral playing among the most meaningful parts of their vocation.

Common Tunes Include:

- *"Just a Closer Walk with Thee"*
- *"I'll Fly Away"*
- *"When the Saints Go Marching In"*
- *"Precious Lord, Take My Hand"*
- *"Old Rugged Cross"*

These songs blend Protestant, Catholic, and African American spiritual traditions.

Musical Funerals as Living Cultural Heritage

For Louisiana communities, musical funerals are more than ritual—they are identity.

They preserve:

- African heritage
- Catholic influence
- Community pride
- Love for the deceased
- The resilience of the living

Even families who rarely participate in other cultural traditions often request musical funerals because of their profound emotional and spiritual resonance.

GROUND LESSONS
Tourism and Tradition

New Orleans jazz funerals have become globally recognized, sometimes attracting tourists. Cemetery Authorities must ensure that ceremonies remain sacred, not turned into spectacles. Respectful boundaries preserve the dignity of the deceased and the community.

Practical Considerations for Cemetery Authorities

Musical funerals require coordination:

- Planning for large crowds
- Managing processional routes
- Accommodating musicians
- Ensuring respectful behavior from bystanders
- Working with Social Aid and Pleasure Clubs
- Maintaining decorum in Catholic sections
- Managing sound levels during other services

Cemetery Authorities who understand the tradition can facilitate the funeral with dignity and pastoral sensitivity.

PASTORAL INSIGHT
"The Music Is Pastoral Care"

For many families, music does what words cannot. It comforts, unites, and heals. Cemetery professionals who embrace this reality become faithful ministers of compassion.

Continuity: The Future of Musical Funerals

Despite changes in culture and urban life, musical funerals remain vibrant. Younger generations continue:

- Joining brass bands
- Participating in second lines
- Honoring ancestors with music
- Blending tradition with modern styles

This continuity ensures that Louisiana's burial culture remains one of the most distinctive in the world.

Conclusion

Musical funerals in Louisiana embody a profound union of faith, culture, and community. They honor grief with honesty, celebrate life with joy, and proclaim resurrection with music that rises from the streets to the heavens.

These traditions stand as a testament to Louisiana's spiritual heritage – one in which the human heart finds expression through melody and in which the Church's hope in eternal life is proclaimed not only in words but also in song.

In the next chapter, we will explore **Pet Interments & Catholic Teaching**, examining how cultural expectations intersect with Catholic doctrine and cemetery responsibilities.

PART V

SPECIAL TOPICS

CHAPTER 15

PET INTERMENTS & CATHOLIC TEACHING

Louisiana families hold deep affection for their pets. In Cajun, Creole, and rural communities, animals are often considered part of the family fabric. They accompany families through joys, hardships, and even moments of grief. It is therefore not uncommon for Cemetery Authorities—especially in Catholic cemeteries—to encounter requests to place the cremated remains of a pet with a deceased loved one or inside a family tomb.

While such requests arise from love, they also raise important questions of Catholic teaching, reverence for sacred ground, and cemetery policy. This chapter explores the Catholic Church's position on human and animal burial, clarifies the distinctions between the two, and offers pastoral guidance for responding compassionately to families.

THE CATHOLIC UNDERSTANDING OF THE HUMAN PERSON

Catholic teaching holds that the human person — body and soul — is made in the image and likeness of God (cf. **Gen 1:27**).

KEY PRINCIPLES:

- The human body is a temple of the Holy Spirit (cf. **1 Cor 6:19**).
- The dignity of the human person is unique and unparalleled (cf. **CCC 1700**).
- Burial rituals honor the body as destined for resurrection (cf. **CCC 990 – 1019**).

Human remains, therefore, have a **distinct theological and moral status**. Cemeteries, especially Catholic ones, exist primarily for the reverent burial of **human persons**.

CULTURAL NOTE
Animals as Family in Louisiana

In Cajun and Creole households, pets often have deep sentimental significance. Stories of loyal hunting dogs, protective farm animals, or beloved household pets are woven into family identity. These emotional realities must be approached with compassion, not dismissal.

THE CATHOLIC VIEW OF ANIMALS

The Church teaches that animals are part of God's creation and that humans owe them kindness and care (cf. **CCC 2416 – 2418**).

However:

- Animals do not possess immortal souls as humans do (cf. **CCC 363**).
- They are not recipients of sacraments.
- They do not share in the resurrection of the body as humans do.

Therefore, **the burial of animals is fundamentally different from the burial of human persons**.

The Church's Position on Pet Interment in Catholic Cemeteries

Catholic cemeteries exist for the burial of baptized and unbaptized human persons, not animals. This is grounded in:

- The theological nature of sacred ground (cf. **CIC 1205 - 1210**).
- The nature of Christian burial (cf. **CIC 1176**).
- The dignity uniquely owed to the human body.

Therefore:

Most Catholic dioceses **do not permit** the burial or interment of pets — whether whole bodies or cremated remains—in a Catholic cemetery, tomb, or columbarium.

This includes:

- Placing pet ashes in a family tomb
- Placing pet ashes in a mausoleum crypt
- Scattering pet ashes on cemetery grounds
- Burying pets in designated pet sections within a Catholic cemetery

Even though some civil cemeteries allow pet interment, Catholic cemeteries must adhere to doctrinal principles.

> **PASTORAL INSIGHT**
> **Clarity with Compassion**
>
> Families often make such requests during moments of grief. A pastoral response should both affirm the family's love for their pet and gently explain the Church's theology: **"We honor the uniqueness of your loved one by reserving this sacred space for human burial."**

Families often make such requests during moments of grief. A pastoral response should both affirm the family's love for their pet and gently explain the Church's theology: **"We honor the uniqueness of your loved one by reserving this sacred space for human burial."**

Legislative and Practical Considerations in Louisiana

Civil cemetery laws in Louisiana (Title 8) do not prohibit the interment of animals on cemetery property unless the Cemetery Authority prohibits it. This means:

- **Civil law may allow it,**
- **But Catholic cemeteries do not,** due to Church teaching.

The cemetery Authority's rules, combined with ecclesiastical oversight, govern what is permitted.

GROUND LESSONS
"Fluffy Should Rest with Mom"

Many families say something like: **"Mom loved her little dog. I want them together."** This is a sincere expression of affection, not theological confusion. Cemetery Authorities should respond gently, explaining that:

- Pets may be buried in a pet cemetery
- Memorialization options exist
- Catholic sacred ground must remain specifically for human remains

The refusal must be pastoral, not punitive.

Why the Church Reserves Consecrated Ground for Humans

Reserving consecrated ground exclusively for human persons expresses:

The Uniqueness of the Human Person

Only humans bear the imago Dei (cf. **CCC 1701**).

Belief in the Resurrection

Cemeteries symbolize the hope of resurrection for the dead (cf. **CCC 997**).

Sacredness of the Human Body

The body is not merely biological matter—it is sacramental.

Consistency of Ritual

Funeral rites are for human persons, not animals.

Clarity of Catholic Identity

Blurring the distinction between human and animal burial risks confusing theological anthropology.

Pet Memorialization Outside the Cemetery

Families can honor their pets in ways that fully respect Catholic teaching:

Options Include:

- Burial or cremation interment in a **pet cemetery**
- Keeping a home memorial (outside Catholic sacred ground)
- Planting a tree or creating a garden shrine
- Displaying a photo in the home
- Including the pet's memory in family stories or scrapbook pages
- Placing a symbolic item in the person's coffin (where permitted), **without** placing pet remains inside

Some families place a small charm, collar tag, or photo of the pet with the deceased–**this is generally allowed**, as it does not equate animal burial with human burial.

> **PASTORAL INSIGHT**
> **Symbolic Tokens Are Allowed**
>
> Many Cemetery Authorities permit families to place a small token representing the pet with the deceased (e.g., a collar tag or photo) **as long as it is not the pet's remains.** This meets the family's emotional needs without violating cemetery regulations.

CULTURAL PRACTICES THAT INFLUENCE PET BURIAL EXPECTATIONS

Some Louisiana families come from traditions – especially rural or coastal areas, where animals are buried on family land or where distinctions between human and animal burial are less formalized.

Additionally:

- Some Protestant communities permit pets to be interred in human cemeteries.
- Secular cemeteries may advertise "companion burials" with pets.

This can lead families to assume the same applies to Catholic cemeteries.

CULTURAL NOTE
Pets as Emotional Anchors

In many Louisiana homes, pets accompany people through illness, isolation, or the aging process. Their deaths can therefore evoke deep grief. Cemetery Authorities must treat such grief with the same compassion accorded to other forms of loss.

Addressing Common Questions

"Can my pet's ashes be placed in my mausoleum crypt?"

No. Catholic cemeteries prohibit the interment of animal remains.

"Can you mix pet ashes with cremated human remains?"

No. This violates the dignity of the human body and the sanctity of Catholic burial.

"Can I scatter my pet's ashes in a Catholic cemetery?"

No. Scattering of any remains – human or animal – is not allowed in Catholic cemeteries.

"Can I place a photo or symbol of my pet in the tomb?"

Yes – within reason, and with cemetery approval. Symbolic items are allowed; remains are not.

"Can I bury my pet on church or parish grounds?"

> Generally, **no**, unless a parish specifically designates an off-site area for pet burial (rare).

Caring for Families in Grief

Families requesting pet burial are expressing love, not irreverence. Pastoral responses should:

- Acknowledge the emotional bond
- Honor the family's grief
- Clarify Catholic teaching
- Offer alternatives
- Express compassion in tone and language
- Avoid legalistic or dismissive replies

Cemetery directors and clergy should be prepared with gentle scripts and written policies.

GROUND LESSONS
"This Is a Place for You, Not Just Your Loved One"

A helpful pastoral approach is to remind families: **"This sacred space is here for you, too. It is where you will pray, remember, and visit. We want it to remain a place focused on human dignity and resurrection."**

Conclusion

Pet interments raise real pastoral and cultural questions in Louisiana cemeteries, where family bonds and Catholic traditions run deep. While the Church prohibits the burial of animals in consecrated ground, compassionate guidance ensures that families feel supported, not judged.

By clearly articulating the theological, pastoral, and practical reasons for this distinction, Cemetery Authorities maintain the sacred identity of Catholic burial grounds while honoring the love and grief that families bring to the heart of their request.

CHAPTER 16

CEMETERY PRESERVATION & SACRED MEMORY

Cemeteries are more than repositories of stone and earth — they are repositories of *memory*, *identity*, and *faith*. A cemetery tells the story of a community: its ancestors, its trials, its devotions, and the enduring love that binds generations across time. In Louisiana, where family, culture, and Catholic faith intertwine so deeply, preserving cemeteries is a sacred responsibility that extends far beyond maintenance. It is a stewardship of history, heritage, and the hope of the Resurrection.

This chapter explores the spiritual meaning of cemetery preservation, the cultural imperatives that undergird it, and the practical challenges faced by Louisiana's sacred burial grounds.

THE SACRED DUTY OF PRESERVING BURIAL GROUNDS

The Catholic Church teaches that cemeteries are sacred spaces because they hold the bodies of those baptized in Christ, destined for resurrection (cf. **CCC 1681 - 1690**).

Preservation is therefore not merely an aesthetic task—it is an act of mercy and reverence.

Three Foundations of Sacred Preservation

1. **Theological**
   The body will rise again (cf. **CCC 997**), and the place where the body rests must honor that truth.
2. **Cultural**
   Cemeteries preserve identity, lineage, and the stories of Louisiana's families.
3. **Pastoral**
   Well-maintained burial grounds provide comfort, dignity, and peace to the living.

> **GROUND LESSONS**
> **"When a Cemetery Dies, Memory Dies"**
>
> Many Louisiana communities have seen old or rural cemeteries fall into neglect. When this happens, the stories of ancestors fade, and the community loses part of itself. Preservation is an act of communal love.

Louisiana's Unique Preservation Challenges

Cemetery preservation in Louisiana carries special difficulties due to:

Weather and Climate

- Humidity
- Subtropical heat
- Heavy rainfall
- High winds
- Intense storms and hurricanes

These conditions accelerate:

- Mold
- Rot
- Crumbling stucco
- Rusted ironwork
- Flooding

Coastal Erosion and Land Loss

Louisiana's coastline is disappearing at alarming rates, threatening historic cemeteries—particularly in tribal, Cajun, and Creole communities.

Vegetation Overgrowth

Vines, moss, and invasive species damage stones and vaults.

Generational Transition

As families move away or grow smaller, old family tombs may fall into disuse.

Historic Burial Practices

Above-ground tombs require:

- Regular whitewashing
- Periodic stucco repairs
- Masonry upkeep

The need for constant care matches their beauty.

CULTURAL NOTE
"The Family Tomb as Heritage"

In Cajun and Creole culture, the family tomb is often passed down as an heirloom. Its preservation symbolizes respect for family lineage and the honoring of ancestors.

The Theology of Sacred Memory

Preservation is intimately tied to Catholic teaching on memory:

- **The communion of saints** (cf. **CCC 946 - 962**)
- **The dignity of the body**
- **Prayer for the dead** (cf. **CCC 1030 - 1032**)
- **The sacredness of burial places** (cf. **CIC 1240 - 1241**)

In this sense, cemetery preservation becomes a living act of faith.

Sacred Memory Means:

- We do not forget our dead.
- We do not abandon their resting places.
- We honor the story they began.
- We preserve our connection to those who shaped us.

In Louisiana, this memory is often expressed through ongoing traditions such as All Saints Day, family tomb cleanings, and annual cemetery blessings.

Practical Preservation: Maintenance and Repair

Cemeteries must be maintained with care, professionalism, and consistency.

Key Preservation Practices:

Masonry and Stucco Repair

- Re-plastering cracks
- Repairing weather damage
- Repainting and whitewashing
- Replacing spalled brick

Cleaning and Vegetation Control

- Removing invasive vines
- Trimming trees
- Clearing walkways
- Safe removal of debris

Drainage and Erosion Management

- Ensuring graves don't flood
- Maintaining culverts and ditches
- Preventing soil loss around tombs

Preservation of Historic Ironwork

- Rust removal
- Repainting
- Refastening aging components

Documentation and Mapping

- Mapping plots and tombs
- Photographing historic structures
- Cataloging inscriptions

This helps preserve heritage even if structures degrade.

PASTORAL INSIGHT
"Preservation Is Evangelization"

A well-maintained cemetery proclaims the Catholic faith to the community. It shows reverence, communicates hope, and invites prayer. Many non-practicing Catholics reconnect with the Church when visiting a well-cared-for cemetery.

Historic Cemeteries and Restoration Efforts

Louisiana is home to some of the oldest Catholic cemeteries in the United States. Preservation efforts often involve:

- Diocesan heritage committees
- Parish volunteers
- Professional conservators
- Local historical societies
- Universities and archaeologists
- Tribal preservation officers
- Grants and state resources

Common Restoration Needs:

- Restoring crumbling tombs
- Repairing historic iron fencing
- Preserving French and Creole inscriptions
- Cleaning stone without damaging patina
- Stabilizing leaning monuments
- Digital archiving of records

CULTURAL NOTE
Community Workdays

Many rural parishes still hold cemetery cleaning days, where families gather to mow, wash tombs, repaint crosses, and care for ancestral graves. This fellowship is preservation in its purest form.

Abandoned, Neglected, and Undocumented Graves

Louisiana's laws **(La. R.S. 8:304 – 306) provide guidance on** abandoned cemeteries and the process for restoring, relocating, or documenting graves when ownership is unclear.

COMMON SCENARIOS INCLUDE:

- Family lines are dying out
- Tombs without clear heirs
- Historic graves left unattended for decades
- Damage from storms or flooding
- Relocation by necessity (e.g., coastal erosion)

CATHOLIC CEMETERIES MUST BALANCE:

- Legal responsibility
- Respect for the dead
- Pastoral sensitivity
- Diocesan policy
- Historical stewardship

Some cemeteries partner with genealogists to identify long-forgotten relatives, restoring dignity through memory.

GROUND LESSONS
"Every Grave Has a Name, Even If We Don't Know It"

When inscriptions fade or markers are lost, cemetery staff must treat every grave with the same reverence as the clearly identified ones. Each person buried is known to God.

Protecting Cemeteries from Vandalism, Theft, and Damage

A sad reality is that cemeteries sometimes face vandalism or theft of:

- Statues
- Bronze vases
- Marble plaques
- Ironwork
- Sacred items

Cemeteries combat this through:

- Surveillance systems
- Lighting improvements
- Fencing
- Community involvement
- Police partnerships
- Immediate repair of desecrated areas

Protection is not merely practical—it is a sacred responsibility (cf. **CIC 1210**).

Natural Disasters and Emergency Response Plans

Louisiana cemeteries face hurricanes, floods, and tornadoes. Preparedness is essential:

Emergency Planning Should Address:

- Securing loose items

- Sandbagging vulnerable areas
- Documenting tombs in advance
- Rapid assessment after storms
- Notification procedures for families
- Coordination with diocesan offices and civil authorities
- Careful handling of displaced vaults or remains (cf. **La. R.S. 8:660 – 662**)

Cemetery Authorities must be trained and ready for disaster.

PASTORAL INSIGHT
The Ministry of Presence After a Disaster

Following catastrophic events, families often come to the cemetery seeking reassurance. A present, compassionate Cemetery Authority becomes a source of stability and consolation.

Preserving Sacred Memory Through Ritual and Tradition

Cemetery preservation is not merely physical—it's spiritual.

Traditions That Preserve Memory Include:

- All Saints' Day blessings
- Rosary processions
- Grave marking ceremonies
- Veteran memorial services
- Candlelight vigils
- Family reunions at tombs

These rituals ensure the cemetery remains a living place of prayer.

Collaboration with Parishes and the Wider Community

Cemetery preservation succeeds when communities work together:

- Parishes adopt historic cemeteries
- Families volunteer during cleanups
- Schools teach students about local burial history
- Scouts perform service projects
- Cultural organizations document oral histories

These partnerships strengthen both heritage and faith.

Conclusion

Preserving cemeteries in Louisiana is both a ministry and a cultural calling. From flood-prone coastal communities to the historic Catholic parishes of Acadiana and the river parishes, cemeteries stand as testaments to the love, faith, and identity of generations.

- To preserve a cemetery is to preserve a story.
- To preserve a story is to preserve a people.
- And to preserve a people is to honor God's work in them—past, present, and future.

The next chapter will explore **Cultural Sensitivity for Cemetery Authorities**, equipping professionals with practical guidance for serving Louisiana's diverse communities with compassion and respect.

CHAPTER 17

CULTURAL SENSITIVITY FOR CEMETERY AUTHORITIES

Cemeteries are places where culture, faith, and memory converge. In Louisiana—where Catholic, Cajun, Creole, African American, Native American, Jewish, Protestant, and immigrant traditions coexist—Cemetery Authorities must serve families with both pastoral sensitivity and professional competence.

A cemetery Authority is not merely a caretaker of land; they are a caretaker of heritage, faith, and human dignity. Cultural sensitivity ensures that each family's burial customs are understood, respected, and carried out in harmony with the cemetery's Catholic identity and the legal framework of Title 8.

This chapter provides practical guidance on how Cemetery Authorities can navigate Louisiana's diverse cultural expectations with grace, equity, and pastoral care.

The Catholic Identity of the Cemetery

Before addressing cultural diversity, a fundamental truth must be clear: **a Catholic cemetery is a sacred space dedicated to Christian burial (cf. CIC 1205 - 1210)**.

Core Principles of Catholic Venue Identity:

- The cemetery is consecrated ground.
- Human remains receive reverent burial consistent with Catholic teaching (cf. **CIC 1176**).
- Public rituals should reflect Christian hope in resurrection.
- Cultural practices are welcome when they are compatible with the sacredness of the space.

Cultural sensitivity does not require compromising Catholic identity. Instead, it guides Cemetery Authorities in welcoming diverse expressions of grief and remembrance within the framework of Catholic teaching.

CULTURAL NOTE
"Many Traditions, One Sacred Ground"

Louisiana families with mixed religious or cultural backgrounds often choose Catholic cemeteries because of heritage ties, not doctrinal precision. Pastoral sensitivity in these situations strengthens relationships and maintains the cemetery's mission.

Understanding Louisiana's Cultural Landscape

Louisiana's burial culture reflects centuries of blending, migration, and memory. Cemetery Authorities routinely interact with families shaped by:

- Cajun French heritage
- Creole cultural traditions
- African American gospel and musical expressions
- Native American ancestral customs
- Catholic devotional practices
- Protestant or interfaith families
- Immigrant traditions (Hispanic, Vietnamese, Honduran, Irish, Italian, etc.)

Each brings expectations, expressions of grief, and traditions that influence burial planning.

Understanding these contexts helps Cemetery Authorities respond effectively.

Principles of Cultural Sensitivity

Listen Before You Lead

Families often reveal their needs simply by telling stories. Listening first:

- Builds trust
- Prevents misunderstandings
- Helps identify what is cultural vs. liturgical
- Allows authorities to guide with clarity

Speak with Compassion and Clarity

Policies should never be expressed coldly or bureaucratically. When delivered pastorally, rules become an act of service.

Distinguish Custom from Doctrine

Many cultural requests can be accommodated *before* or *after* the Catholic rites.
This preserves both tradition and Catholic liturgical integrity.

Respect Family Emotion

Grief heightens cultural attachment. Sensitivity is crucial when discouraging items or activities not permitted on sacred ground.

Apply Rules Consistently

Cultural sensitivity does not mean cultural favoritism. Consistency fosters fairness and prevents confusion.

PASTORAL INSIGHT
"Your Heritage Belongs Here Too"

A welcoming tone communicates that the cemetery is not a museum of Catholic uniformity – it is a sacred home where diverse families can express their love for their dead in ways that are faithful and dignified.

Common Cultural Situations and How to Navigate Them

Musical Funerals and Second Lines

- Many African American and Creole families expect music at the cemetery.
- Allowed: Hymns, gospel songs, brass music *after* the committal rite.
- Not allowed: Loud music during the liturgical rite or inside columbaria.
- Strategy: Offer clear timing guidelines.

Large, Extended Families

Cajun, Creole, and African American families may gather in large numbers.

Authorities should:

- Prepare for crowd control
- Allow for longer graveside gatherings
- Coordinate with clergy regarding timing
- Provide extra chairs or shade when possible

Hospitality communicates respect.

Cultural Grave Decorations

Some families place:

- Wreaths
- Colorful artificial flowers
- Memorial objects representing the deceased's hobbies
- French or Creole inscriptions
- Tribal symbols

Permissible when:

- Safe
- Weatherworthy
- Not contrary to Catholic identity
- Do not impede maintenance

Photos with Glass Fronts

Glass poses a safety hazard and must be strictly prohibited. Provide guidance toward durable, porcelain alternatives.

Ancestor Honoring by Native American Families

Native families may seek to:

- Place symbolic items
- Burn incense before the liturgical rite
- Offer tribal songs or prayers

Accommodate cultural expressions **outside the ritual proper.** Clarify boundaries with sensitivity.

Requests to Scatter Ashes

Prohibited in Catholic cemeteries (cf. *Ad resurgendum cum Christo*, 2016). Explain with compassion and offer dignified alternatives.

Mixed-Faith Families

Some services blend Catholic, Protestant, or secular elements.

- The Catholic liturgy must conform to Catholic norms.
- Other elements may occur *before or after*, in coordination with the clergy.

Pet Burial Requests

As treated in Chapter 15:

- Prohibited for theological reasons
- Allow symbolic tokens only
- Respond with compassion and alternatives

> **GROUND LESSONS**
> **"We Always Did It This Way Back Home"**
>
> Families often cite historical customs — sometimes practiced in civil or rural cemeteries. Use these moments to educate gently about the Catholic identity of sacred ground.

Communication Strategies for Cultural Sensitivity

Provide Written Policies

Clear written guidelines prevent conflict.

Review Policies at the Time of Purchase

Families absorb information better before emotions are high.

Provide Scripted Explanations

Cemetery staff should have prepared pastoral responses for sensitive topics.

Offer Compromise Solutions

Example:
"While we cannot allow scattering, we can inter the cremated remains with appropriate dignity."

Affirm Cultural Identity Whenever Possible

Small gestures—pronouncing names correctly, recognizing traditions, acknowledging family heritage—build trust.

PASTORAL INSIGHT
"Not Everything Is a Battle"

Many cultural practices are easily accommodated. Reserve firm boundaries for issues that truly affect sacred space, theology, or public safety.

Avoiding Cultural Pitfalls

Cemetery Authorities must be aware of:

Cultural Stereotyping

Never assume a family's traditions based on appearance or surname.

Imposing Cultural Uniformity

Policies should maintain dignity, not suppress culture.

Disrespectful Language

Avoid dismissive or technical phrasing during emotional conversations.

Inflexibility Where Flexibility Is Allowed

Not every issue is doctrinal; some depend on the Cemetery Authority's discretion.

Ignoring Historical Marginalization

African American and Native communities, in particular, may carry historical wounds regarding burial inequality. Sensitivity in these contexts is crucial.

Training Staff in Cultural Awareness

A culturally sensitive cemetery is shaped not only by policy but by people.

TRAINING SHOULD INCLUDE:

- Overview of local cultural traditions
- Review of Catholic burial theology
- Scripts for common sensitive scenarios
- Customer service training
- Guidelines for dealing with grief
- Safety and emergency protocol

Well-trained staff are essential to preserving the cemetery's dignity and mission.

CULTURAL SENSITIVITY AND TITLE 8 COMPLIANCE

Cultural accommodation must always align with:

- Louisiana Revised Statutes Title 8
- Diocesan policy
- Cemetery rules
- Safety obligations
- Respect for sacred ground

Cultural expectations cannot override:

- Burial permitting requirements
- Mausoleum entombment regulations
- Interment rights procedures
- Disinterment rules
- Prohibitions on scattering
- Prohibitions on non-human remains
- Safety provisions
- Public order standards

Consistency ensures legal protection and pastoral fairness.

Cultural Sensitivity as Evangelization

When Cemetery Authorities serve families with cultural respect:

- Hearts open
- Trust grows
- Family relationships deepen
- People return to the cemetery for prayer
- The Church's presence is strengthened

A cemetery can become a place of evangelization—not through preaching, but through compassion.

CULTURAL NOTE
"Hospitality Is the First Language of Louisiana"

When families feel welcomed, they recognize the cemetery not as an institution but as a sacred home.

CONCLUSION

Cultural sensitivity is not a challenge to Catholic cemeteries—it is a gift.
By honoring the rich tapestry of Louisiana traditions, Cemetery Authorities become ministers of compassion who serve families at one of the most vulnerable moments of their lives.

Cultural awareness strengthens:

- Catholic identity
- Community relationships
- Legal compliance
- The beauty and dignity of sacred ground

In the next chapter, we will discuss establishing working relationships with clergy and how to prevent miscommunication and help services go smoothly for families.

CHAPTER 18

WORKING WITH CLERGY

Catholic cemeteries do not exist in isolation — they exist in relationship with the Church. Clergy serve as shepherds of the faithful, teachers of doctrine, and guardians of the sacred rites surrounding death and burial. Cemetery Authorities, in turn, serve as stewards of the sacred ground where those rites are ultimately fulfilled.

When clergy and Cemetery Authorities work together, the Church's care for the dead becomes beautifully unified, pastoral, and dignified. But when communication breaks down, confusion, conflict, and pastoral strain can arise for grieving families. This chapter provides guidance on forming strong relationships with clergy to ensure that Catholic burial practices are carried out with reverence, clarity, and cooperation.

THE SHARED MISSION: CARE FOR THE DEAD AND THE LIVING

Both clergy and Cemetery Authorities share a common mission rooted in Catholic teaching:

- **To honor the dignity of the human body** (cf. **CCC 2300**)
- **To comfort the grieving** (cf. **CCC 1681 - 1690**)
- **To maintain sacred spaces** (cf. **CIC 1205 - 1210**)

- **To proclaim the hope of the Resurrection** (cf. 1 Cor 15:20–22)
- **To preserve Catholic identity and tradition**

Clergy do so through the liturgy, sacraments, and pastoral counsel. Cemetery Authorities do so through stewardship of the burial grounds, compassion toward families, and faithful adherence to Title 8 and diocesan norms.

Both roles are indispensable.

CULTURAL NOTE
The Clergy-Cemetery Bond in Louisiana

In Louisiana's historic parishes, the cemetery was often directly behind the church. Priests knew every family by name, and cemetery traditions were intertwined with parish life. Many families still expect this closeness today — even when cemeteries are corporate or diocesan rather than parish-owned.

The Role of Clergy in Catholic Burial

Clergy provide:

- **Sacramental care:** Anointing, Viaticum, Confession
- **Funeral rites:** Vigil, Funeral Mass, and Rite of Committal
- **Pastoral counseling**
- **Guidance during grief**
- **Catechesis on Catholic burial norms**
- **Blessing of graves and cemeteries**

Their presence brings meaning, structure, and hope to the burial process.

Cemetery Authorities should understand the clergy's responsibilities to support them effectively.

The Role of the Cemetery Authority

Cemetery professionals contribute by:

- Preparing and maintaining the burial space
- Ensuring procedures comply with Title 8
- Coordinating burial logistics
- Supporting families with compassion
- Maintaining the sacred dignity of the cemetery
- Assisting with All Saints' Day blessings and processions
- Preserving parish and diocesan heritage

Clergy depend on Cemetery Authorities for organization, clarity, and reliability.

PASTORAL INSIGHT
"Our Ministries Converge at the Grave"

The cemetery is the final chapter of the Church's ministry to the deceased. Clergy lead the rites. Cemetery Authorities protect the place where those rites conclude.

Communication: The Essential Ingredient

Clear communication between clergy and Cemetery Authorities prevents confusion and ensures pastoral excellence.

Important Communication Touchpoints:

1. **Funeral Scheduling**
    - Confirm the time of interment before the Mass is scheduled.
    - Ensure clergy know the burial location and any logistical details.
- **Special Circumstances**
    - Cremation before Mass
    - Multiple burials
    - Burial of a child or stillborn infant
    - Burial of a non-Catholic relative
- **Cultural Requests**
    - Music
    - Processions
    - Family rituals
    - Decorations
    - Extended family gatherings
- **Complex Family Situations**
    - Estranged relatives
    - Multiple claimants to a space
    - Title ownership disputes

Clergy should never be surprised at the cemetery.

GROUND LESSONS
The "Clergy Didn't Know" Problem

Funeral chaos usually arises when:

- Families tell clergy one thing,
- Tell the funeral home another,
- And tell the cemetery something different.

Cemetery Authorities can prevent conflict by taking the lead in verification.

Working with Deacons

Deacons frequently conduct:

- Vigil services
- Rosaries
- Rite of Committal
- Cemetery blessings
- Pastoral visits to grieving families

Deacons often serve as a bridge between priests and Cemetery Authorities. Maintain a strong relationship with deacons – they are essential partners in pastoral burial care and can frequently fill in when priests are unavailable.

Special Pastoral Situations and the Role of Clergy

Burial of an Unbaptized Infant or Stillborn Child

- Catholic rite available (Order of Christian Funerals)
- Cemetery staff must communicate with clergy immediately
- Sensitivity is paramount

Burial of a Non-Practicing Catholic

- Clergy may still perform the rites unless the person publicly opposed the Church (cf. **CIC 1184**). Cemetery Authorities should avoid making theological judgments.

Burial of a Non-Catholic Relative

- Allowed in Catholic cemeteries.
- Clergy involvement varies by circumstance.

Complex or High-Emotion Funerals

- Sudden or traumatic deaths
- Homicides
- Suicides
- Deaths of young persons
- High-publicity funerals

Cemetery Authorities must collaborate closely with clergy for pastoral and logistical reasons.

Liturgical and Non-Liturgical Boundaries

Cemetery Authorities must understand:

What Clergy Control:

- All elements of the Rite of Committal
- All liturgical prayers and blessings
- All sacramental and ecclesiastical decisions

What Cemetery Authorities Control:

- Timing and logistics of interment
- Safety and operations of cemetery property
- Decoration and conduct policies
- Space usage and disposition rights
- Legal compliance

Clear boundaries prevent conflict.

PASTORAL INSIGHT
"Respect Expertise"

Clergy are experts in theology and liturgy. Cemetery Authorities are experts in burial law, logistics, and cemetery governance. Mutual respect improves everything.

Louisiana's Cultural Realities: Supporting Clergy

Clergy who are new to Louisiana – or new to parish ministry –may not be familiar with:

- All Saints' Day customs
- French or Creole rosaries
- Cajun family structures
- Second lines or brass band funerals
- Native American burial expectations
- Title 8 Cemetery Regulations

Cemetery Authorities can help significantly by educating clergy on local customs in advance.

CULTURAL NOTE
Priests from Abroad

Louisiana relies heavily on priests from Africa, India, and Latin America.
These priests bring rich faith but may be unfamiliar with:

- Above-ground tombs
- Cremation placement in family vaults
- Louisiana's cultural funeral expectations
- Complex Cajun surnames

Gentle guidance prevents misunderstandings and strengthens pastoral ministry.

Annual and Seasonal Collaboration

All Saints Day

- Coordinate with clergy for the blessing of graves
- Provide maps, water, and sound equipment
- Manage crowds and parking
- Prepare the cemetery in advance

Lenten and November Devotions

- Way of the Cross in the cemetery
- Memorial Masses
- All Souls' candlelight services

Veterans' Day Observances

- Flag placement
- Special prayers
- Orchestration of military honors

Strong cooperation ensures spiritual richness and safety.

Avoiding Conflicts and Navigating Disagreements

Conflicts may arise over:

- Scheduling disputes
- Cultural requests
- Miscommunication
- Unexpected family issues
- Decoration or conduct violations
- Sensitive theological concerns

Key Principles for Conflict Resolution:

1. **Assume goodwill**
2. **Seek clarity, not blame**
3. **Protect the family from internal conflict**
4. **Maintain professionalism**
5. **Document decisions when necessary**
6. **Keep the bishop or pastor informed in extreme situations**

Cemetery Authorities should never publicly contradict clergy, and clergy should respect cemetery rules.

GROUND LESSONS
"When Clergy Ask for What the Cemetery Can't Allow"

Occasionally, clergy may request something contrary to cemetery policy—for example, allowing a glass-encased memorial, or permitting a burial without proper Title 8 documentation. Handle these moments with:

- Respect
- Clarity
- Written policy in hand
- Follow up with the pastor or diocesan authorities if needed.

Mutual Formation: Learning from Each Other

Clergy benefit from understanding:

- Louisiana Title 8 requirements
- Cemetery governance
- Burial rights and ownership
- Interment vs. inurnment
- Mausoleum procedures
- Safety considerations

Cemetery Authorities benefit from understanding:

- Catholic liturgy
- Ritual timing
- Pastoral dynamics
- Sacramental theology
- Funerary etiquette

Regular meetings build shared knowledge.

The Cemetery Authority as Pastoral Minister

Cemetery professionals often serve families before clergy do. Their words carry pastoral weight.

Cemetery Authorities minister by:

- Listening
- Guiding families through grief
- Clarifying Catholic burial norms
- Supporting clergy
- Embodying compassion in every interaction

When Cemetery Authorities embrace this identity, the work becomes not just administrative but evangelical.

Conclusion

Working with clergy is both an art and a ministry. Together, clergy and Cemetery Authorities form a pastoral partnership that accompanies families from the moment of death to the final act of committal.

When cooperation is strong:

- The funeral rites unfold smoothly
- Families feel comforted and supported
- The cemetery maintains its sacred character
- The Church's mission is fulfilled with dignity

In the next chapter, we move to bringing law, culture, and pastoral care together into a comprehensive framework.

CHAPTER 19

MANAGING CULTURAL TRADITIONS WITHIN TITLE 8

Louisiana's cemeteries sit at the crossroads of faith, culture, and law. Families bring deeply rooted traditions—Catholic, Cajun, Creole, African-American, Native American, and immigrant customs – to the burial of their loved ones. Cemetery Authorities must honor these traditions while ensuring that every burial, procession, and memorial practice complies with Louisiana Revised Statutes Title 8 and with the cemetery's Catholic identity.

This chapter offers practical tools, pastoral guidance, and legal clarity for navigating cultural expectations within the framework of Catholic norms and civil cemetery law.

THE ESSENTIAL BALANCE

Effective cemetery management rests on three interconnected responsibilities:

CATHOLIC IDENTITY

Catholic cemeteries are sacred places dedicated to the burial of human persons (cf. **CIC 1205 - 1210**). The rites performed here proclaim the hope of the Resurrection (cf. **CIC 1176; CCC 1680 - 1690**).

Cultural Sensitivity

Louisiana families express grief through music, prayer, language, processions, and decoration. These traditions are meaningful and deserve respect when compatible with Catholic teaching.

Legal Compliance (Title 8)

Louisiana Revised Statutes Title 8 governs:

- Interment rights
- Burial authorization
- Disinterment and reinterment
- Mausoleum and columbarium operation
- Abandoned or neglected cemeteries
- Cemetery maintenance
- Recordkeeping and trust funds

Cultural practices must fit within this legal framework.

PASTORAL INSIGHT
"Culture Is Not the Enemy of Order."

Most cultural requests can be accommodated safely, legally, and reverently. Boundaries matter, but explaining them with compassion matters even more.

General Principles for Cultural Accommodation

Principle 1 – What Is Not Forbidden May Often Be Allowed

Most cultural customs – songs, rosaries, French prayers, decorations – are fully compatible with Catholic burial.

Principle 2 – Culture Must Not Alter the Sacred Rites

The Church's liturgical rites must remain intact. Cultural elements belong:

- **Before** the Rite of Committal
- **After** the Rite of Committal
- **Never inside** the liturgical text

Principle 3 – Title 8 Controls Burial Decisions

Only interment right holders may authorize a burial (**La. R.S. 8:803 - 805**).

Principle 4 – Safety and Maintenance Are Non-Negotiable

For example:

- No glass photo frames
- No decorations blocking walkways
- No open flames unless permitted and supervised

Principle 5 – Consistency Builds Trust

Families accept boundaries more easily when rules are applied fairly.

Cultural Traditions Common in Louisiana Funerals

Louisiana's diverse traditions often include:

- Brass bands or gospel music
- French rosaries
- Creole hymns
- Second lines
- Tribal songs or symbolic items
- Extended family gatherings at the graveside
- Colorful wreaths or cultural decorations
- Family stories or testimonies before committal

Most of these can be permitted, provided they respect:

- The liturgical structure
- Cemetery safety
- Title 8 requirements
- The sacred character of the space

CULTURAL NOTE
Music as Memory

Gospel choirs, French hymns, and brass dirges are not disruptions – they are expressions of Louisiana's soul. Properly timed, they enrich the cemetery's sacred atmosphere.

Applying Title 8 to Cultural Situations

Burial Authorization

Cultural expectations do **not** override legal requirements:

- The interment rights owner controls burial decisions.
- Extended family influence cannot supersede Title 8.

Cremation Practices

Title 8 allows cremation, but Catholic teaching requires:

- Permanent placement
- No scattering
- No dividing ashes
- No mixing human and pet remains
  (*Ad resurgendum cum Christo*, 2016)

Processions and Music

Music is allowed:

- Before or after the rite
- Not during the liturgical prayers
- Not in a way that disrupts other burials

Decorations

Permitted:

- Durable flowers
- Cultural symbols compatible with Catholic identity
- Flags, rosaries, and statues

Restricted:

- Glass items
- Invasive or breakable decorations
- Non-Christian ritual objects
- Items impeding maintenance

Native American Traditions

Allow:

- Symbolic items
- Tribal prayers before/after the rite
- Cultural textiles or art

Prohibit:

- Rituals incompatible with Catholic teaching
- Open-flame or smoke-based rituals, unless approved
- Ground disturbance without authorization

African American Traditions

Allow:

- Gospel hymns
- Brass band dirges
- Celebration music *after* the committal
- Extended family participation

Maintain:

- Respectful volume
- Clear timing guidance

Immigrant Community Traditions

Vietnamese, Honduran, Mexican, Filipino, and Irish traditions may include:

- Incense
- Family altars
- Cultural hymns

Accommodate outside the liturgy and within safety guidelines.

Managing Conflict: Cultural vs. Legal vs. Liturgical Expectations

Families may feel tension between:

- What they want
- What culture expects
- What Church permits
- What Title 8 requires

Keys to Defusing Conflict:

1. **Acknowledge the tradition's importance**
2. **Explain the rule or law clearly**
3. **Offer an alternative**
4. **Maintain a compassionate tone**
5. **Never contradict clergy publicly**
6. **Document issues when necessary**

GROUND LESSONS
"Who Gets to Decide?"

Disputes often arise when:

- Cousins or siblings want to override the spouse
- Adult children disagree among themselves
- Family tradition contradicts legal ownership

Title 8 protects the cemetery:

Only the legally authorized person may decide.

Preventing Problems Before They Begin

Provide Written Policies — Give families rules at the time of plot purchase.

Train Staff in Cultural Awareness — Brief scripts and role-play prepare staff for sensitive situations.

Meet with Clergy Regularly

Align on:

- Music
- Processions
- Ritual boundaries
- Cemetery expectations

Communicate with Funeral Homes

Ensure:

- Timing
- Paperwork
- Cultural expectations
- Clergy arrival

  Consistency across all parties.

Safety, Decorum, and the Sacred Character of the Cemetery

Regardless of culture or custom, cemeteries must remain:

- Safe
- Orderly
- Reverent
- Dignified

Title 8 obligates cemeteries to maintain grounds in good condition (**La. R.S. 8:903**). The Catholic identity obligates them to maintain a sacred atmosphere.

Cultural expression must always enhance—not diminish—the cemetery's atmosphere of prayer.

Cultural Accommodation as Ministry

Accommodating cultural practice is not merely good customer service — it is:

- Pastoral care
- Evangelization
- Respect for heritage
- A ministry of compassion

Families often remember kindness at the cemetery long after the funeral.

Conclusion

Louisiana's cemeteries are living reflections of faith, law, and culture. Managing cultural traditions within Title 8 requires:

- Clear legal understanding
- Strong pastoral sensitivity
- Respect for Catholic identity
- Flexible but consistent policies
- Compassionate communication

When done well, Cemetery Authorities honor the dead, support the living, and preserve the rich traditions that make Louisiana's burial culture unique.

This chapter completes the framework for cemetery professionals to serve competently, with cultural awareness, and with Christian charity.

CONCLUSION

Cemeteries are places of memory, culture, and hope. To walk among Louisiana's burial grounds — whether the white-washed tombs of Acadiana, the storied cemeteries of New Orleans, the quiet family plots of rural parishes, or the sacred resting places of Native and African American ancestors — is to encounter a living history of the people who shaped this land. Our cemeteries tell the story of Louisiana: the blending of French and Spanish traditions, African and Caribbean spirituality, indigenous reverence for ancestors, Catholic theology, and the daily lived faith of countless families.

Throughout this book, we have explored not only the customs that appear at gravesides, but **the deeper meaning behind them** — a meaning rooted in human dignity, cultural identity, and Christian hope. The Catholic understanding of burial is not merely a ritual obligation; it is an act of love toward the living and the dead. It speaks to the truth that the human body, even after death, participates in the mystery of Christ's Resurrection. Our cultural traditions — whether sung in French, Creole, English, drums, brass, fiddle, or whispered prayer — become the vessels through which this hope is expressed.

Louisiana is unique in the United States for the way it has preserved and integrated these traditions. Here, grief is rarely quiet or expressionless. Instead, it is embraced as part of life, part of family, part of culture — whether through a rosary prayed in old Cajun French, a jazz procession carrying a loved one home, or a circle of hands gathered around a family tomb. Each expression, in its own way, is a proclamation that *death does not speak the final word.*

Yet alongside this cultural richness stands the practical and sometimes challenging work of cemetery leadership. Burial rights, Title 8 compliance, clergy collaboration, maintenance obligations, safety policies, and family communication all form part of the sacred duty entrusted to cemetery directors. Those who care for the dead and their resting places serve families at their most vulnerable moments. They stand at the intersection of law, culture, and faith—navigating sorrow, expectation, conflict, and tradition with reverence and compassion.

As a Catholic Cemetery Director, I have learned that **good cemetery ministry is always a balance**:

- **honoring culture without compromising faith**,
- **upholding law without losing charity**,
- **maintaining order while respecting grief**, and
- **protecting sacred ground while welcoming human hearts.**

The cemetery is a classroom of humility and wisdom. It teaches patience. It teaches respect. It teaches us that no two families mourn in the same way — and that cultural traditions, when received with understanding, can be powerful instruments of healing. Whether a cemetery is Catholic, interdenominational, municipal, or private, the lessons of cultural sensitivity and theological integrity remain the same: every person deserves to be remembered, mourned, and buried with dignity.

As we conclude this book, we return to the promise at the heart of Christian burial: **that life is changed, not ended; that the body sown in weakness will be raised in glory; that love does not cease at the grave.**

Louisiana's burial traditions – Catholic, Cajun, Creole, African American, Native, Jewish, Protestant, and beyond – each carry this promise in its own language. They remind us that the cemetery is not merely a place of death, but a place of faith, culture, and continuity. Families return year after year not only to grieve, but to tell stories, light candles, sing hymns, and keep memories alive. Here, the past and present meet. Here, the living and the dead remain bound in communion.

May this book serve as a guide, a companion, and a tribute to the sacred work of burial in Louisiana.

May it strengthen the hands of cemetery directors, inform the minds of students and researchers, and comfort the hearts of families.

And may it help preserve the extraordinary traditions that make Louisiana's burial culture not only unique, but profoundly beautiful.

As caretakers of sacred ground, we stand together with generations before us and generations yet to come—guardians of memory, servants of hope, and witnesses to the promise of eternal life.

Amen.

GENERAL INDEX

A

B

C

D

E

F

G

H

I

J

K

L

M

N

O

P

Q

R

S

Made in United States
Orlando, FL
04 November 2026

90207821R00138